# MAC N' CHEESE
# TO THE RESCUE

**101 Recipes to Spice Up Everyone's
Favorite Boxed Comfort Food**

Kristen Kuchar

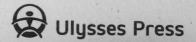

Ulysses Press

Published by:
Ulysses Press
P.O. Box 3440
Berkeley, CA 94703
www.ulyssespress.com

A Hollan Publishing, Inc. Concept

ISBN: 978-1-61243-168-0
Library of Congress Catalog Number 2013931794

Printed in Canada by Marquis Book Printing

10 9 8 7 6 5 4 3 2 1

Acquisitions editor: Keith Riegert
Managing editor: Claire Chun
Editor: Susan Lang
Proofreader: Elyce Berrigan-Dunlop
Production: Jake Flaherty, Lindsay Tamura
Design: what!design @ whatweb.com
Cover photos: skillet mac n' cheese © Hollan Publishing; dry macaroni
    © Harm Kruyshaar/Shutterstock.com

Distributed by Publishers Group West

*To Doctor Mark, because it's you and me versus.*

# TABLE OF CONTENTS

# ACKNOWLEDGMENTS

This has been such an amazing experience, and I would like to thank Ulysses Press for the opportunity to share my love for cooking. I would especially like to thank my wonderful publicist, Kourtney Joy, who was a joy to work with and made the process stress-free and upbeat.

Most of all, I am ever grateful to my irreplaceable, phenomenal husband, Mark Kuchar. He has been a silent force in this book as well as everywhere else in my life. I may be the creative "idea man," but it's his intelligence, strong focus, and work ethic that give all of my ideas wings.

Thank you for always having faith in me, for helping me create the life I dreamed of, and for being such a loyal, fun partner on this journey. Food is my passion, but it always seems to taste a little better when I'm eating with you.

# INTRODUCTION

It's funny how I can trace mac n' cheese throughout the course of much of my life. I remember, as a kid, sitting at my best friend Sarah's kitchen table eating fun-shaped mac n' cheese and laughing so hard it hurt. I'll never forget lounging in my college dorm room trying to figure out chemistry and life over a microwaved orange-powder version of mac (still working on both, by the way). Possibly the most unforgettable memory is of the gourmet lobster mac n' cheese I was indulging in when my boyfriend asked me to be his wife.

It's not surprising that mac n' cheese is such a classic staple and the ideal comfort food. But it's also a blank canvas. Those simple truths, as well as my lifelong fondness for mac n' cheese, were the inspiration for this book. Yes, noodles smothered in gooey cheese is good on its own, but it's even better with an extra pop. This book takes a convenience food and explores other ingredients and flavors, uses leftovers, and, most importantly, creates inventive, exciting meals and snacks from a food we all know and love.

## Cooking Mac n' Cheese

In developing the recipes for this book, I did not use one particular brand of mac n' cheese, although all came from a box. You can just as easily use freshly cooked or leftover homemade mac n' cheese with these recipes. Some recipes specifically call for a certain type of mac n' cheese or specify the shape of noodle or the or type of cheese. If a recipe is not specific, then feel free to use whatever type of mac n' cheese you'd like. Here are the three basic types that I used.

## Deluxe Mac n' Cheese

When I use the term "deluxe," I am referring to the boxed mac n' cheese that comes with a cheese sauce. Cooking directions will vary by brand, but in general here's how you make deluxe mac n' cheese.

In a large pot over high heat, bring 6 to 8 cups of water to a boil. Once the water is at a boil, add 1 teaspoon of sea salt. Then add the noodles. Cook the noodles for 8 to 10 minutes or until they reach the desired consistency. The cooking time will depend on the size and shape of the noodles. Whenever a recipe calls for additional cooking or baking, keep in mind that the noodles will continue to cook. For this reason, you may want to stick to the shorter amount of time. While the noodles are cooking, stir occasionally. Drain the noodles in a colander, and do not rinse. Return the noodles to the pot, add the packet of cheese, and stir.

## Regular Mac n' Cheese

When I don't specify a type of mac n' cheese (the ingredient list will read "1 box mac n' cheese"), I am talking about a box that comes with a powder packet and usually requires butter and milk or water to make the sauce. Generally, here's how to cook regular mac n' cheese.

In a large pot over high heat, bring 6 to 8 cups of water to a boil. Add the noodles. Cook the noodles, stirring occasionally, for 7 to 8 minutes depending on the desired consistency, shape of the noodle, and brand directions. Drain the noodles, and do not rinse. Pour the noodles back into the pot. Although brands vary, many call for ¼ cup of milk and 4 tablespoons of butter.

## Microwavable Mac n' Cheese

Wherever there's a microwave oven—at home or in a work lunchroom, dorm room, or motor inn—microwavable mac n' cheese can come in handy when you're looking for a filling meal or just a quick snack. Place the macaroni and the designated amount of water in the microwavable dish and cook for the directed length of time. Remove from the microwave oven, add the cheese powder, and stir until the cheese dissolves.

Many recipes in this book can be turned into microwavable recipes. Simply reduce the additional ingredients to suit your desired amount. You can easily steam vegetables in a microwave oven, and use precooked meats to combine with the microwaved mac n' cheese.

# BREAKFAST

Mac n' cheese may be a go-to for lunch or dinner, but it probably isn't the first thing you think of for your morning meal. But adding mac n' cheese to favorites like bacon, sausage, and eggs gives breakfast an exciting twist. These breakfast recipes are all easy to make, and the added mac makes them hearty and satisfying. Prepare these when you want to serve something memorable at a brunch.

# FIESTA OMELET

*This dish features such great ethnic and savory flavor that I don't limit it to just breakfast. It's also a great choice for lunch, brunch, or dinner. For extra heat, I like to top the omelet with a dash of hot sauce or salsa, and you can opt for sour cream if you like.* **Serves 4 to 5**

1 box deluxe mac n' cheese

7 ounces chorizo, casing removed

1 small onion, chopped

1 tablespoon jarred jalapeño or 1 fresh jalapeño, seeded and chopped

6 large eggs, beaten

¼ teaspoon garlic salt

⅛ teaspoon black pepper

1¼ cups shredded cheddar cheese or Mexican cheese blend (5 ounces), divided

**1.** Preheat the oven to 375°F. Cook the mac n' cheese as directed, and set aside.

**2.** Meanwhile, in a large nonstick skillet over medium-high heat, cook the chorizo, stirring occasionally with a rubber spatula, about 7 minutes. As the sausage cooks, break it up with the spatula. Turn the heat down to medium-low and add the onion and jalapeño. Cook on low, stirring occasionally, until the onion is translucent and the jalapeño is softened, about 15 minutes.

**3.** In a large bowl, thoroughly combine the beaten eggs, garlic salt, black pepper, cooked mac n' cheese, chorizo mixture, and ¼ cup cheddar cheese or Mexican cheese blend, and transfer to a greased 9 x 13-inch baking dish. Top with the remaining 1 cup of cheese and cover with aluminum foil. Bake until the egg is fully cooked, about 30 minutes. Remove the cover, and bake until the top has slightly browned, an additional 3 to 5 minutes.

• • • • • • • • •

# MILE-HIGH CITY OMELET

*I love bacon, but sometimes ham is a nice alternative at breakfast. I make this dish whenever I have leftover ham from the previous night's dinner or if I have lunch meat that I want to use up.* **Serves 4 to 5**

1 box sharp cheddar mac n' cheese

1 tablespoon olive oil

1 small onion, chopped

½ medium green bell pepper, chopped

1½ cups chopped leftover cooked ham or ham steak

6 large eggs, beaten

1 cup shredded cheddar cheese (4 ounces)

**1.** Preheat the oven to 375°F. Cook the mac n' cheese as directed, and set aside.

**2.** Meanwhile, heat the olive oil in a large skillet over medium-low heat. Add the onion and bell pepper and cook, stirring occasionally, until tender, about 10 minutes. Add the chopped ham, and cook, stirring occasionally, until heated through, about 2 minutes.

**3.** In a large bowl, thoroughly combine the beaten eggs, cooked mac n' cheese, ham mixture, and cheddar cheese, and transfer to a greased 9 x 13-inch baking dish. Cover with aluminum foil. Bake until the egg is fully cooked, about 30 minutes. Remove the cover, until the top has slightly browned, and bake an additional 3 to 5 minutes.

• • • • • • • •

# GOOD MORNING MAC N' CHEESE

*Hash browns can get a little boring after a while, so this recipe substitutes a heartier option—mac n' cheese. This is a great breakfast dish to make for a crowd.* **Serves 4 to 5**

1 box deluxe mac n' cheese

1 (8-ounce) package breakfast sausages

6 large eggs, beaten

½ cup chopped scallions, green and white parts

1 cup shredded cheddar cheese (4 ounces)

**1.** Preheat the oven to 375°F. Cook the mac n' cheese as directed, and set aside.

**2.** Meanwhile, in a large nonstick skillet, cook the breakfast sausages as directed. Once the sausages are cooked, chop them into small pieces.

**3.** In a large bowl, thoroughly combine the beaten eggs, cooked mac n' cheese, cooked sausage, scallions, and cheddar cheese. Transfer to a greased 9 x 13-inch baking dish and cover with aluminum foil. Bake until the egg is fully cooked, about 30 minutes. Remove the cover, and bake until the top has slightly browned, an additional 3 to 5 minutes.

* * * * * * * *

# MY BIG FAT GREEK OMELET

*The salty bite of feta makes this dish pop. I throw any leftovers inside a pita pocket and eat it for lunch.* **Serves 4 to 5**

1 box deluxe mac n' cheese

1 tablespoon olive oil

1 (8-ounce) package spinach

6 eggs, beaten

½ cup crumbled feta cheese (2 ounces)

**1.** Preheat the oven to 375°F. Cook the mac n' cheese as directed, and set aside.

**2.** Meanwhile, heat the olive oil in a large skillet over medium-low heat. Cook the spinach, stirring occasionally, until tender, 5 to 7 minutes.

**3.** In a large bowl, thoroughly combine the beaten eggs, cooked mac n' cheese, cooked spinach, and feta cheese. Transfer to a greased 9 x 13-inch baking dish and cover with aluminum foil. Bake until the egg is fully cooked, about 30 minutes. Remove the cover, and bake until the top has slightly browned, an additional 3 to 5 minutes.

• • • • • • • • •

# STEAK PESTO EGGS

*When I was growing up, my dad always wanted to go out for breakfast, and his favorite dish was steak and eggs. Having steak for breakfast seemed like a treat to me, so whenever I have leftover steak, I make this dish and remember my dad.* **Serves 4 to 5**

1 box deluxe four-cheese mac n' cheese

6 large eggs, beaten

2 cups chopped, cooked leftover steak

¼ cup pesto

1 cup shredded mozzarella cheese (4 ounces)

**1.** Preheat the oven to 375°F. Cook the mac n' cheese as directed.

**2.** Mix together the beaten eggs, cooked mac n' cheese, leftover steak, pesto, and mozzarella cheese until well incorporated. Transfer to a greased 9 x 13-inch baking dish and cover with aluminum foil. Bake until the egg is fully cooked, about 30 minutes. Remove the cover, and bake until the top has slightly browned, an additional 3 to 5 minutes.

· · · · · · · · ·

# WAKE UP PHILLY OMELET

*Besides cooking, traveling is my favorite pastime. And one of the best American regional dishes I've ever tasted is the iconic Philly cheese steak. The orange Cheez Whiz that tops the sandwich reminds me of mac n' cheese, so this recipe was a natural when I came home from my last trip to Philadelphia. This is a great way to use any leftover cooked steak you may have.* **Serves 4 to 5**

1 box shell mac n' cheese

1 tablespoon olive oil

2 cups chopped, cooked steak

1 small onion, chopped

½ medium green bell pepper, chopped

½ medium red bell pepper, chopped

6 large eggs, beaten

½ cup pepper jack cheese (2 ounces)

**1.** Preheat the oven to 375°F. Cook the mac n' and cheese as directed, and set aside.

**2.** Meanwhile, heat the olive oil in a large skillet over medium-high heat. Add the cooked steak, onion, and bell peppers and cook, stirring occasionally, until the onion and peppers are tender, 5 to 8 minutes.

**3.** In a large bowl, thoroughly combine the beaten eggs, cooked mac n' cheese, steak and vegetable mixture, and pepper jack cheese. Transfer to a greased 9 x 13-inch baking dish and cover with aluminum foil. Bake until the egg is fully cooked, about 30 minutes. Remove the cover, and bake until the top has slightly browned, an additional 3 to 5 minutes.

# BACON OMELET

*Bacon and eggs is an iconic breakfast dish, but even it can gain from a little added excitement. To bulk it up while giving it a twist, why not add mac n' cheese?* **Serves 4 to 5**

1 box mac n' cheese

8 ounces bacon (½ package)

6 large eggs, beaten

1½ cups shredded cheddar cheese (6 ounces), divided

⅛ to ¼ teaspoon black pepper

**1.** Preheat the oven to 375°F. Cook the mac n' cheese as directed, and set aside.

**2.** Meanwhile, in a large nonstick skillet over medium-high heat, cook the bacon, turning when crisp on the underside, until cooked through and crisp on both sides, 10 to 15 minutes. Remove and drain on paper towels. Once the bacon has cooled, crumble it into small pieces.

**3.** In a large bowl, mix together the beaten eggs, crumbled bacon, cooked mac n' cheese, and 1 cup shredded cheddar until well incorporated. Transfer to a 9 x 13-inch baking dish and top with the remaining ½ cup cheddar. Cover with aluminum foil. Bake until the egg is fully cooked, about 30 minutes. Remove the cover, and bake until the top has slightly browned, an additional 3 to 5 minutes.

• • • • • • • •

# BUON GIORNO OMELET

Buon giorno *simply means "good morning" in Italian, and with this inspired breakfast it will be. Pancetta is similar to bacon except it's not smoked. It is cooked the same way bacon is and can be found in most grocery stores. For the cheese, you can use any Italian cheese blend such as one containing Parmesan, Asiago, and Romano.* **Serves 4 to 5**

1 box mac n' cheese

¼ pound pancetta, sliced

6 eggs, beaten

1 teaspoon Italian seasoning blend

1½ cups shredded Italian cheese blend (6 ounces), divided

**1.** Preheat the oven to 375°F. Cook the mac n' cheese as directed, and set aside.

**2.** Meanwhile, in a large nonstick skillet over medium-high heat, fry the pancetta slices, turning when crisp on the underside, until crispy and golden brown, 5 to 8 minutes. Remove and drain on paper towels. Once the pancetta has cooled, crumble it into small pieces.

**3.** Mix together the beaten eggs, crumbled pancetta, cooked mac n' cheese, Italian seasoning, and 1 cup shredded Italian cheese blend until well incorporated. Transfer to a greased 9 x 13-inch baking dish and top with the remaining ½ cup Italian cheese blend. Cover with aluminum foil. Bake until the egg is fully cooked, about 30 minutes. Remove the cover, and bake until the top has slightly browned, an additional 3 to 5 minutes.

· · · · · · · ·

# HEALTHY START OMELET

*Whenever I know I'm in for a full day of physical activity, I start off with this healthy breakfast to get the fuel I need. The vegetables I use vary, depending on what I have on hand. Many different cheeses work well with this dish, such as cheddar, mozzarella, or a blend of several varieties.* **Serves 4 to 5**

6 slices turkey bacon

1 tablespoon butter

½ cup chopped green bell pepper

½ cup chopped red bell pepper

½ cup chopped onion

1 box whole wheat mac n' cheese

1 cup egg whites (from about 6 large eggs)

¼ teaspoon black pepper

¼ teaspoon garlic powder

1 cup reduced-fat cheese (4 ounces), divided

**1.** Preheat the oven to 375°F.

**2.** In a large nonstick skillet over medium-high heat, cook the turkey bacon, turning when crisp on the underside, until cooked through and crisp on both sides, 8 to 10 minutes. Remove and drain on paper towels. Once the turkey bacon has cooled, crumble it into small pieces.

**3.** Melt the butter in a small skillet over medium-low heat. Add the bell peppers and onion and cook, stirring occasionally, until the vegetables are softened and the onion is translucent, about 10 minutes.

**4.** While the vegetables are cooking, prepare the mac n' cheese as directed.

**5.** In a large bowl, thoroughly combine the egg whites, cooked mac n' cheese, cooked vegetables, black pepper, garlic powder, and ½ cup reduced-fat cheese, and transfer to a greased 9 x 13-inch baking dish. Top with the remaining ½ cup cheese, and cover with aluminum foil. Bake until the egg is fully cooked, about 30 minutes. Remove the cover, and bake until the top has slightly browned, an additional 3 to 5 minutes.

• • • • • • • • •

# SNACKS AND APPETIZERS

I love serving snacks and appetizers sometimes in place of one big meal. This way you get to have a variety of options. These snacks are fantastic for a group of guests, or even as the start to a family meal. Better yet, many of these recipes use leftover mac n' cheese, so it gives mac remaining from other dishes a whole new taste. Whether it's for a crunchy, spicy jalepeño mac ball or the familiar flavor of a classic corn dog coating, you won't believe a box of mac n' cheese can create these appetizers.

# CHICKEN MAC-ADILLA

*Anytime I clean out my fridge, I end up making quesadillas to use up
ingredients, including leftover mac n' cheese. Use whatever type of
Mexican cheese you like or have on hand along with your other favorite
ingredients. I like taco-size tortillas for this recipe, but you can use
whatever size you prefer and adjust the amount of filling ingredients
accordingly.* **Serves 1**

½ tablespoon vegetable oil,
divided

2 (6-inch) corn or flour tortillas

⅓ cup shredded Mexican cheese
blend (about 1½ ounces)

¼ cup leftover cooked mac n'
cheese

pinch of cumin or taco seasoning

sprinkle of onion, cilantro,
jalapeño, or tomato, ¼ cup total

¼ cup sour cream or salsa, for
topping

**1.** Brush a small skillet lightly with oil, and heat over medium-
high heat. You need only enough oil so the tortilla doesn't
stick or burn. Place one tortilla in the skillet. Add a sprinkle of
Mexican cheese, followed by the cooked mac n' cheese, and
top with your favorite quesadilla ingredients such as onion,
cilantro, jalapeños, and seasoning. Finish with another sprinkle
of Mexican cheese and the remaining tortilla.

**2.** Let the bottom tortilla brown and the cheese start to melt
before you carefully turn the quesadilla to the other side. It's
done when the cheese has melted and both tortillas have
browned. You can use a pizza cutter to slice the quesadilla. To
serve, top with salsa or sour cream.

**3.** Repeat for additional servings.

●　●　●　●　●　●　●　●　●

# TACO PARTY

*The best part of this dish is that it's so versatile. You can use beef, turkey, or chicken. Then for toppings, you can use whatever you have on hand, whatever's on special at the grocer's, or your favorite ingredients. Serve with tortilla chips for a fun party food.* **Serves 5 to 6**

1 box deluxe mac n' cheese

1 pound ground beef, ground turkey, or ground chicken

½ cup water

1 (1-ounce) packet taco seasoning

Optional toppings: shredded lettuce, chopped tomato, chopped onion, refried beans, sour cream, tortilla chips

**1.** Cook the mac n' cheese as directed, and set aside.

**2.** In a large nonstick skillet over medium-high heat, brown the ground meat, breaking it into small pieces with a wooden spoon. Cook until browned and cooked through, about 10 minutes. Drain off the fat. Add the water and taco seasoning, stirring well, and cook for another 5 minutes. Remove from the heat and add the cooked mac n' cheese to the seasoned ground meat, stirring until well mixed.

**3.** Turn the ground meat and mac n' cheese mixture onto a large serving plate, and layer the lettuce, tomato, onion, refried beans, and sour cream—or your favorite taco toppings—on top. Serve with tortilla chips.

• • • • • • • • •

# MINI MAC MEATBALLS

*Leftover mac n' cheese can be transformed into these mini meatballs, which are great as an appetizer, as a snack, in a sandwich, or even as a meal with a salad.* **Serves 5 or 6**

1 pound ground chuck

⅛ cup grated Parmesan cheese (½ ounce)

¼ cup finely chopped green bell pepper

¼ cup Italian-style bread crumbs

1 large egg, beaten

1 teaspoon garlic salt

1 teaspoon black pepper

2 cups leftover cooked mac n' cheese

**1.** Preheat the oven to 350°F. In a large bowl, use your hands to combine all the ingredients thoroughly but gently. Do not overmix. Form into golf ball–size meatballs. Brown the meatballs in a large nonstick skillet over medium-high heat. Turn so each side browns, a total of about 15 minutes.

**2.** Once the meatballs are fully browned, transfer them to an ungreased cookie sheet. Bake until fully cooked, about 20 minutes.

· · · · · · · · ·

# SPICY MAC BALLS

*These crispy bites are irresistible and easy to make for a party or other get-together. My favorite part is that you can dip them in whatever you like. Try marinara sauce, ranch dressing, or spicy ketchup dip—just add a dash of cayenne to regular ketchup.* **Serves 6 or 7**

1 large egg

1¾ cups panko bread crumbs, divided

¼ teaspoon garlic salt

¼ teaspoon black pepper

2 cups leftover cooked mac n' cheese

¼ cup shredded cheddar cheese (1 ounce)

1 tablespoon minced jalapeño

2 tablespoons canola or other oil suitable for frying

**1.** In a small bowl, beat the egg and set aside. On a plate, mix 1½ cups bread crumbs with the garlic salt and black pepper, and set aside.

**2.** In a large bowl, combine the leftover mac n' cheese, cheddar cheese, jalapeño, and remaining ¼ cup bread crumbs. Form golf ball–size balls. Roll each ball in the beaten egg, and let any drippings fall off. Then roll in the seasoned bread crumbs. Set each ball aside.

**3.** Heat the oil in a large skillet over medium-high heat. Once the oil is hot, place the balls in the pan. Let each side brown before carefully turning the balls. Once all sides are brown and crispy, remove the balls with a slotted spoon, and place on paper towels or on a cooling rack to let the oil drain. Serve with your favorite dipping sauce.

· · · · · · · · ·

# STUFFED MUSHROOMS

*I love making stuffed mushrooms as an appetizer because they're a nice change from chips and dips. Use cremini mushrooms, sometimes called baby portobellos, for bite-size hors d'oeuvres that can be served at parties. Choose fully grown creminis, or portobellos, if you want to make a side dish for a meal.* **Serves 6 or 7**

1½ teaspoons olive oil

¼ cup finely chopped onion

2 cloves garlic, finely chopped

1 cup leftover cooked or frozen, thawed, and drained spinach

¼ cup grated Parmesan cheese (1 ounce), divided

1 cup leftover cooked mac n' cheese

8 ounces cremini mushrooms

⅛ cup Italian-style bread crumbs

**1.** Preheat the oven to 350°F. Heat the oil in a large skillet over medium heat. Cook the onion and garlic, stirring occasionally, until they start to soften, about 5 minutes. Add the spinach and continue to cook an additional 5 minutes. Remove from heat.

**2.** Once the spinach mixture has cooled, add ⅛ cup Parmesan cheese and the leftover mac n' cheese, and combine well. Remove the mushroom stems and spoon the spinach mixture into the mushroom caps. Sprinkle the tops with the remaining ⅛ cup Parmesan cheese and the bread crumbs. Place in an ungreased baking dish. Bake uncovered until the bread crumbs start to brown and the mushrooms are slightly softened, about 20 minutes.

· · · · · · · · ·

# MINI MAC BURGERS

*You don't have to make these burgers miniature, but it's a great opportunity to make fun appetizers with varied toppings. Besides the traditional ketchup and mustard toppings, think outside the box with crumbled tortilla chips, barbecue sauce, or Gorgonzola cheese.* **Serves 5 or 6**

1 pound ground beef or ground turkey

1 cup leftover cooked mac n' cheese

1 teaspoon garlic salt

1 teaspoon onion powder

½ tablespoon Worcestershire sauce

1 teaspoon black pepper

1 tablespoon ketchup

1 large egg, beaten

buns

**1.** In a large bowl, thoroughly but gently combine the ground meat, leftover mac n' cheese, garlic salt, onion powder, Worcestershire sauce, black pepper, ketchup, and egg. Do not overmix. Form into mini patties.

**2.** Place the burgers on a hot grill or in a large nonstick skillet over medium-high heat, and cook to desired doneness. Ground turkey should be fully cooked, and ground beef should be at least pink in the center. Grill or toast the buns. Use the toppings of your choice on the burgers.

• • • • • • • • •

# BRUSCHETTA MAC

*Bruschetta is my favorite appetizer since it's so simple to make. The basil in my version imparts such a fresh taste, and the mac n' cheese gives it a twist as well as makes it a little heartier.* **Serves 6**

½ baguette or crusty long loaf bread, sliced ½-inch thick (12 pieces)

2 tablespoons olive oil

3 teaspoons Italian seasoning blend, divided

1 cup leftover cooked mac n' cheese

1 teaspoon balsamic vinegar

1 teaspoon garlic salt

1 clove garlic, minced

5 basil leaves, chopped

3 tablespoons chopped tomato

1 tablespoon grated Parmesan cheese

**1.** Preheat the oven to 400°F. Lightly brush one side of each baguette slice with olive oil and ¼ teaspoon of Italian seasoning. Place on an ungreased cookie sheet, and bake until the bread starts to crisp and turn slightly brown, 5 to 8 minutes. Let cool completely.

**2.** In a medium bowl, mix together the mac n' cheese, balsamic vinegar, garlic salt, garlic, basil, and tomato. Spread on the cooled baguette slices. Sprinkle Parmesan cheese over the top.

· · · · · · · · ·

# JALAPEÑO MAC CORN BREAD

*The mac n' cheese in the corn bread keeps the bread moist and the jalapeño gives it a kick. I love to serve this corn bread with chili, meat loaf, and gumbo. To make things easier, I grab a box of corn bread mix that can be found with other bread and cake mixes on grocery shelves.* **Serves 8**

1 (16-ounce) package corn bread mix

¼ cup finely minced seeded jalapeño

1½ cups shredded cheddar cheese (6 ounces), divided

1 cup leftover cooked mac n' cheese

¼ cup chopped scallions or chives

**1.** Preheat the oven to 350°F. In a large bowl, prepare the corn bread mix batter as directed. Add in the jalapeño, ½ cup cheddar cheese, and the mac n' cheese, stirring until well combined.

**2.** Transfer to the type of baking dish recommended on the corn bread mix package. Sprinkle the chopped scallions or chives over the top. Then top with the remaining 1 cup cheddar cheese. Bake uncovered according to the package directions, or until the top is golden brown and a knife comes out of the bread clean.

* * * * * * * *

# BOARDWALK MAC

*These little bites have the same delicious, soft, and crispy coating of a classic corn dog. Get a group together to watch a baseball game and serve these bites while the hot dogs and burgers are on the grill.*

**Serves 5 to 6**

about 1 cup canola or other oil suitable for frying

1 cup flour

1 cup cornmeal

¼ cup granulated sugar

1 tablespoon baking powder

1 cup milk

2 large eggs, beaten, divided

2 cups leftover cooked mac n' cheese

**1.** Preheat the oil in large skillet over medium-high heat. Meanwhile, in a large bowl, combine the flour, cornmeal, sugar, and baking powder. Then add the milk and one beaten egg, and mix well to form a batter.

**2.** In a separate large bowl, pour the remaining beaten egg over the mac n' cheese. Mash up the noodles slightly with your hands and form into golf ball–size rounds. Dunk the balls in the batter until fully coated.

**3.** Test to be sure the oil is hot by dropping in a small amount of batter. If the batter fries immediately and doesn't sink to the bottom of the oil, the oil is ready. Place the balls in the hot oil. Leave enough room so you can easily turn the balls. Brown them on all sides. Remove with a slotted spoon, and place on paper towels or a cooling rack to let the oil drain.

• • • • • • • • •

# ZEN ROLLS

*The robust Asian flavors of these rolls are unexpected with mac n' cheese but give this dish an exotic feel. I keep frozen shrimp on hand to throw into pasta, rice, omelets, and this dish as well.* **Serves 5**

½ cup chopped cooked shrimp

½ tablespoon chopped fresh cilantro

½ tablespoon chopped fresh basil

1 tablespoon chopped scallions

2 cups leftover cooked mac n' cheese

¼ tablespoon soy sauce

¼ tablespoon sweet-and-sour sauce

10 wonton wrappers or rice paper sheets

**1.** In a large bowl, mix together the shrimp, cilantro, basil, scallions, and mac n' cheese. Pour the soy sauce and sweet-and-sour sauce over the mixture, and toss until coated.

**2.** If using rice paper, soak the sheets in water to soften. Working with one wonton wrapper or rice paper at a time, spoon 1 tablespoon of the mixture onto the center. Fold the edges over the filling and roll tightly.

**3.** If using wonton wrappers, layer wraps onto a cookie sheet. Put wontons into an oven preheated to 450°F. Cook until brown, about 15 minutes. Rice paper does not require cooking.

· · · · · · · ·

# SOUPS AND SALADS

Even though soups and salads are usually served as first-course dishes, adding mac n' cheese to these recipes makes them an entire meal on their own. Classic soups get a revamp with mac n' cheese in the mix. Salad ingredients like slightly sweet apples or crunchy croutons are unexpected accompaniments to the mac that blend together deliciously.

# CHICKEN MAC-TILLA SOUP

*The recipe provides all the comfort of chicken soup but with a spicy kick. I love the bright, fresh flavor of cilantro so I always top it off with a little extra.* **Serves 6 to 8**

2 cups water

2 (15-ounce) cans chicken broth

½ cup chopped green bell pepper

½ cup chopped red bell pepper

2 cloves garlic, finely chopped

½ cup chopped onion

¼ teaspoon paprika

⅛ teaspoon cayenne pepper

¼ teaspoon black pepper

¼ teaspoon onion powder

¼ teaspoon garlic salt

¼ teaspoon cumin

1½ cups shredded leftover cooked chicken

1 cup leftover cooked mac n' cheese

1 cup chopped fresh cilantro

3 to 4 cups sour cream (¼ cup per serving)

3 to 4 cups tortilla chips (½ cup per serving)

**1.** In a large pot over high heat, combine the water and chicken broth. Add the bell peppers, garlic, onion, paprika, cayenne pepper, black pepper, onion powder, garlic salt, and cumin. Bring to a boil. Reduce the heat to medium-low, then simmer uncovered until the vegetables start to soften, about 30 minutes.

**2.** Stir in the chicken and continue to simmer for an additional 10 minutes. Then stir in the mac n' cheese and cilantro. Ladle into serving bowls and top with a dollop of sour cream. Serve with tortilla chips and sour cream.

• • • • • • • •

# MAC-ESTRONE SOUP

*The cheese in the mac n' cheese gives my version of minestrone a silky texture. You can switch out the vegetables to use whichever ones you like best or whatever you have on hand in the refrigerator.* **Serves 6 to 8**

2 cups water

2 (15-ounce) cans beef broth

1 (15-ounce) can diced tomatoes

1 medium zucchini, diced

1 medium red bell pepper, diced

1 medium carrot, diced

1 rib celery, diced

1 teaspoon Italian seasoning blend

1 teaspoon dried oregano

1 teaspoon garlic salt

1 teaspoon onion powder

1 teaspoon black pepper

1 teaspoon white pepper

1 (15-ounce) can kidney beans, drained and rinsed

1 cup leftover cooked mac n' cheese

**1.** In a large pot over high heat, combine the water, beef broth, and tomatoes. Stir in the diced bell pepper, carrot, and celery along with the Italian seasoning, oregano, garlic salt, onion powder, black pepper, and white pepper. Bring to a boil. Reduce the heat to medium-low, then simmer uncovered until the vegetables become soft, about 30 minutes. Add the beans. Stir in the mac n' cheese and cook for an additional 5 minutes. To serve, ladle into bowls.

• • • • • • • • •

# TOMATO SOUP

*Dipping a grilled cheese sandwich into tomato soup is a tradition my husband and I have kept for many years, so adding mac n' cheese to the creamy soup makes perfect sense.* **Serves 6 to 8**

2 (10-ounce) cans tomato soup

1 cup water

1 cup heavy cream

1 cup leftover cooked mac n' cheese

**1.** Combine the canned soup, water, and cream in a large pot over medium-low heat. Cook uncovered, stirring often, until thoroughly heated. Then add the mac n' cheese, and cook for an additional 5 minutes. To serve, ladle into bowls.

* * * * * * * * *

# CHICKEN MAC SOUP

*Transform plain old chicken broth with the addition of leftover chicken and leftover mac n' cheese. This soup couldn't be easier to make—and there's nothing more comforting on a cold day.* **Serves 6 to 8**

2 (15-ounce) cans chicken broth

2 cups water

1 teaspoon garlic salt

1 teaspoon black pepper

½ cup fresh parsley or 1 tablespoon dried parsley

2 medium carrots, diced

2 ribs celery, diced

½ cup diced onion

2 cups shredded leftover cooked chicken

1 cup leftover cooked mac n' cheese

**1.** Combine the chicken broth, water, garlic salt, black pepper, and parsley in a large pot over high heat. Add the diced carrot, celery, and onion. Bring to a boil. Reduce the heat to low, and continue to cook uncovered until the vegetables start to soften, about 30 minutes.

**2.** Add the chicken and continue cooking on low for an additional 10 minutes. Then stir in the mac n' cheese, and cook for another 5 minutes. Ladle into serving bowls.

• • • • • • • • •

# BROCCOLI CHEDDAR SOUP

*It seems as if broccoli is always finding its way onto my plate when I eat mac n' cheese, so the combination of both ingredients in a rich soup is heaven to me.* **Serves 6 to 8**

1 tablespoon butter

1 small onion, chopped

¼ teaspoon onion powder

¼ teaspoon paprika

1 teaspoon black pepper

1 (16-ounce) package frozen broccoli or 4 cups of fresh broccoli florets

1 (10-ounce) can condensed cream of broccoli soup

2 cups milk

1½ cups water

1 cup leftover cooked mac n' cheese

1 cup shredded sharp cheddar cheese (4 ounces), plus more for topping

**1.** In a large pot over medium-low heat, start melting the butter and then add the onion. Cook, stirring occasionally, until translucent, about 10 minutes. Add the onion powder, paprika, and black pepper. Stir in the broccoli, and then add the canned soup, milk, and water. Bring to a boil over medium-high heat, then reduce the heat to medium-low. Continue to cook, stirring occasionally, for about 30 minutes.

**2.** Once the broccoli is at the desired texture, stir in the leftover cooked mac n' cheese. Cook for 5 minutes, stirring occasionally. Add the cheddar cheese until well mixed. Ladle into serving bowls, and top with extra cheese.

• • • • • • • •

# CAJUN COUNTRY GUMBO

*The hot spices in andouille sausage, a staple of New Orleans cuisine, make it my favorite. I'll take any excuse to cook it, and this is one of the best ways.* **Serves 6 to 8**

1 tablespoon butter

5 ounces andouille sausage (about 1 link), casing removed, chopped

½ cup chopped onion

½ cup chopped green bell pepper

½ cup chopped red bell pepper

1 rib celery, chopped

1 teaspoon garlic salt

1 teaspoon black pepper

1 teaspoon white pepper

1 teaspoon onion powder

5 cloves garlic, chopped

1 (14-ounce) can diced tomatoes with juice

2 cups water

2 cups beef broth

½ cup cooked shrimp

1 cup shredded leftover cooked chicken

1 cup frozen and thawed chopped okra

1 cup leftover cooked mac n' cheese

**1.** In a large pot over medium heat, start melting the butter and then add the chopped andouille sausage. Stir frequently until the sausage begins to brown, about 7 to 8 minutes. Add the onion, bell peppers, and celery, and continue to cook, stirring occasionally, for 5 minutes.

**2.** Stir in the garlic salt, black pepper, white pepper, onion powder, chopped garlic, tomato, water, and beef broth. Turn the heat down to low and continue to cook for an additional 10 minutes.

**3.** Add the shrimp, chicken, and okra. Continue to simmer for another 10 minutes. Stir in the mac n' cheese until well incorporated. To serve, ladle into bowls.

• • • • • • • • •

# LOADED MAC SOUP

*Loaded baked potatoes as a side dish and potato skins as an appetizer are such popular choices that extending the concept to soup is almost too good to be true! If you're not familiar with a loaded potato, it's simply a potato literally loaded with delicious toppings, usually including cheese, sour cream, scallions, and bacon. It's like a potato skin with more potato and less skin.* **Serves 6 to 8**

8 ounces bacon (½ package)

2 cups milk

2 (10-ounce) cans condensed cream of potato soup

1 cup chopped scallions, divided

1 teaspoon garlic salt

1 teaspoon black pepper

1 teaspoon onion powder

2 cups shredded extra-sharp cheddar cheese (8 ounces), divided

1 cup leftover cooked mac n' cheese

¼ cup sour cream per bowl

**1.** In a large nonstick skillet over medium-high heat, cook the bacon, turning when crisp on the underside, until cooked through and crisp on both sides, 10 to 15 minutes. Remove and drain on paper towels. Once the bacon has cooled, crumble it into small pieces.

**2.** In a large pot over medium heat, combine the milk, canned soup, ½ cup scallions, garlic salt, black pepper, and onion powder. Cook, stirring often, for 10 minutes. Once the mixture is hot, add half of the cooked bacon and 1 cup cheddar cheese. Stir until the cheese has melted. Add the mac n' cheese, stirring until it is well incorporated.

**3.** Ladle into bowls and sprinkle on the remaining cheddar cheese, cooked bacon, and scallions. Top with a dollop of sour cream.

• • • • • • • • •

# THE BIG APPLE SALAD

*I love the way the tang from the blue cheese contrasts with the slight sweetness of the apple. Amazingly, the mac n' cheese ties those ingredients together.* **Serves 3 or 4**

1 box mac n' cheese

8 ounces bacon (½ package)

1 tablespoon olive oil

½ medium onion, chopped

1 medium Gala apple, chopped

¼ cup crumbled blue cheese (1 ounce)

**1.** Cook the mac n' cheese as directed, and set aside.

**2.** In a large nonstick skillet over medium-high heat, cook the bacon, turning when crisp on the underside, until cooked through and crisp on both sides, 10 to 15 minutes. Remove and drain on paper towels. Once the bacon has cooled, crumble it into small pieces.

**3.** Heat the olive oil in a clean large skillet over medium-low heat. Add the onion and cook, stirring occasionally, for 5 minutes. Add the apple and cook, stirring occasionally, for an additional 10 minutes. Once the apple is slightly soft, transfer the mixture to a large bowl. Stir in the crumbled bacon, hot mac n' cheese, and blue cheese. Serve immediately.

• • • • • • • •

# COBB SALAD

*I love blue cheese in this dish, but if you want something a little less intense, opt for Gorgonzola or even feta. Instead of regular bacon, you may want to try turkey bacon as a healthier option.* **Serves 3 or 4**

1 box mac n' cheese

3 thick slices bacon or ½ cup bacon bits

1 cup shredded or chopped leftover cooked chicken

1 cup crumbled blue cheese (4 ounces)

2 medium ripe avocados, diced

**1.** Cook the mac n' cheese as directed, and set aside to cool.

**2.** If cooking bacon slices rather than using bacon bits, place in a large nonstick skillet over medium heat. Cook the bacon, turning until crisp on the underside, until cooked through and crisp on both sides, 10 to 12 minutes. Remove and drain on paper towels. Once the bacon has cooled, crumble it into small pieces.

**3.** Layer the cooled mac n' cheese with the chicken, bacon, and blue cheese. Top with avocado chunks.

· · · · · · · · ·

# CHICKEN CAESAR

*The croutons add such an unexpected but delightful crunch to this great spin on a favorite salad, which makes an unbeatable side dish for a summer barbecue.* **Serves 4 or 5**

1 box mac n' cheese

2 cups shredded leftover cooked chicken

½ cup grated Parmesan cheese (2 ounces)

1½ cups Caesar dressing

2 cups croutons of choice

**1.** Cook the mac n' cheese as directed, and set aside.

**2.** Once the mac n' cheese is at room temperature, add the chicken, Parmesan cheese, and dressing, stirring until well mixed. Top with croutons and serve.

. . . . . . . . .

# SANDWICHES, PIZZAS, TACOS, AND BURRITOS

When you're craving a little more than a snack but still want something totally unexpected from mac n' cheese, these are the recipes to visit. Putting mac n' cheese on a pizza or in a sandwich or taco combines our favorite cheesy comfort food with a meal that's filling but easy to eat. Many of these recipes don't use the entire box of mac n' cheese, so it's perfect for using up leftovers or making multiple dishes from just one box.

# COWBOY PIZZA

*After having traveled through the South and developing a love for barbecue sauce, I'm always trying to think of unconventional recipes where I can smother my food with it. Since this recipe doesn't use a whole box of mac n' cheese, it's perfect for leftovers. Besides the mac, it's ideal for leftover chicken too.* **Serves 5**

2 tablespoons olive oil

2 medium onions, thinly sliced

1 cup barbecue sauce

1 prepared pizza dough

1 cup leftover cooked mac n' cheese

1 cup shredded leftover cooked chicken

1 cup shredded cheddar cheese (4 ounces)

½ cup chopped chives (optional)

**1.** Preheat the oven to 425°F. Heat the oil in a medium skillet over medium-low heat. Cook the onion, stirring occasionally, until translucent, about 20 minutes. Stir in the barbecue sauce.

**2.** To roll out the pizza dough, cover your work surface lightly with flour to prevent the dough from sticking to the surface. Using a rolling pin, roll the dough to the desired thickness. Transfer to an ungreased baking sheet.

**3.** Spread the onion and barbecue mixture on the pizza dough. Then layer on the mac n' cheese and shredded chicken. Top with the cheddar cheese. Place the baking sheet in the oven and bake for about 15 minutes. Remove from the oven when the crust has slightly browned and the cheese has melted. If desired, sprinkle chopped chives over the top.

· · · · · · · · ·

# ZA-MAC

*I live in Chicago so I have renowned pizza at my fingertips from hundreds of fantastic restaurants. But I still enjoy making this recipe because it reminds me of making little English muffin pizzas when I was a kid and topping them with pepperoni. It's still just as fun making this pizza, and mac n' cheese just adds to the experience.* **Serves 5**

1 prepared pizza dough

1 cup pizza or tomato sauce

1 cup leftover cooked mac n' cheese

1 (8-ounce) package sliced pepperoni

1 cup shredded mozzarella cheese (4 ounces)

**1.** Preheat the oven to 425°F. To roll out the pizza dough, cover your work surface lightly with flour to prevent the dough from sticking to the surface. Using a rolling pin, roll the dough to the desired thickness. Transfer to an ungreased baking sheet.

**2.** Spread the pizza or tomato sauce on the pizza dough. Evenly distribute the mac n' cheese, and dot with pepperoni slices. Top with the mozzarella cheese. Place the baking sheet in the oven and bake for about 15 minutes. Remove from the oven when the crust has slightly browned and the cheese has melted.

* * * * * * * *

# BUFFALO CHICKEN PIZZA MAC

*Serving buffalo wings to friends who are over at your place watching football makes perfect sense. But wings can be messy and rough to eat. This pizza incorporates the goodness of wings and is easier to tuck into.* **Serves 5**

1 prepared pizza dough

1 cup shredded leftover cooked chicken

½ cup buffalo sauce

1 cup leftover cooked mac n' cheese

¼ cup crumbled blue cheese (1 ounce)

½ cup pepper jack cheese (2 ounces)

¼ cup minced celery

**1.** Preheat the oven to 425°F. To roll out the pizza dough, cover your work surface lightly with flour to prevent the dough from sticking to the surface. Using a rolling pin, roll the dough to the desired thickness. Transfer to an ungreased baking sheet.

**2.** In a medium bowl, toss the chicken in buffalo sauce so it's evenly coated. Spread the coated chicken on the pizza dough. Layer the mac n' cheese over the chicken, and top with the blue cheese and pepper jack cheese. Place the baking sheet in the oven and bake for about 15 minutes. Remove from the oven when the crust has slightly browned and the cheese has melted. Sprinkle the celery over the top.

* * * * * * * *

# NOT YOUR MAMA'S GRILLED CHEESE

*Your mom might be cool, but chances are she wasn't cool enough to put mac n' cheese on a classic grilled cheese sandwich. I prefer crusty Italian bread and sharp cheddar, but you can use any type of bread and cheese you'd like. Thinly sliced apple adds a bit of texture to the sandwich.* **Serves 1**

2 thick slices bread

1 tablespoon butter

2 slices cheese

4 thin slices green apple

¼ cup leftover cooked mac n' cheese

**1.** Butter one side of each slice of bread. Layer one slice of cheese, the apple, the mac n' cheese, and the second slice of cheese on the unbuttered side of one slice of bread. Top with the other slice of bread, buttered side out.

**2.** In a medium skillet on medium-low heat, cook the sandwich until the bread has browned and the cheese has melted, 3 to 5 minutes on each side.

• • • • • • • • •

# BALLPARK MAC

*You don't have to be a kid to appreciate a classic hot dog served with mac n' cheese. Tying the two together with a croissant makes this dish easy to serve at a party. I serve it with Spicy Ketchup to give it more of an adult feel.* **Serves 5**

1 (8-ounce) tube croissants

6 to 10 hot dogs, depending on number of croissants

1¼ cups leftover cooked mac n' cheese, divided

**1.** Preheat the oven to the temperature as directed on the package of croissants. Separate the croissants and place on an ungreased baking sheet. Place one hot dog diagonally on each croissant dough. Add ¼ cup leftover mac n' cheese over each hot dog.

**2.** Roll the croissant dough over the hot dog and mac n' cheese, and bake until the croissants have browned, about 10 minutes.

## SPICY KETCHUP

½ cup ketchup

1 tablespoon Sriracha hot sauce

Mix the ketchup and hot sauce for a spicy twist on the basic condiment.

• • • • • • • •

# WEST COAST CLUB

*I love a good spin on a turkey club, and a California theme does the
trick. Slightly peppery arugula and avocado make this club seem as if it
came straight from the West Coast.* **Serves 6**

1 box mac n' cheese

1 pound turkey bacon (1
package)

1½ cups chopped arugula

2 medium tomatoes, chopped

2 medium avocados, chopped

**1.** Cook the mac n' cheese as directed, and set aside.

**2.** In a large nonstick skillet over medium-high heat, cook the
turkey bacon, turning when crisp on the underside, until cooked
through and crisp on both sides, 10 to 15 minutes. Remove and
drain on paper towels. Once the bacon has cooled, crumble it
into small pieces.

**3.** Mix together the bacon and the mac n' cheese. Layer the
mixture in a serving dish. Top with the arugula, tomato, and
avocado.

• • • • • • • • •

# WINDY CITY MAC

*My hometown serves up some pretty noteworthy grub, and my personal favorite is the Italian beef sandwich. And just like the sandwich, my version with mac n' cheese incorporates crunchy, spicy Italian pickled vegetables called giardiniera. Italian beef, a favorite in Chicago, is often simply roast beef seasoned with Italian herbs and can be purchased at Italian delis or markets, or at some grocery stores.* **Serves 5**

1 box mac n' cheese

1 pound thinly sliced cooked Italian beef or roast beef

½ cup giardiniera

1 cup shredded mozzarella or provolone cheese (4 ounces)

**1.** Preheat the oven to 425°F. Cook the mac n' cheese as directed, and set aside.

**2.** Mix together the beef, giardiniera, and mac n' cheese. Transfer to a 9 x 13-inch baking dish, and top with mozzarella or provolone cheese. Bake uncovered until the cheese has melted and slightly browned, about 10 minutes.

• • • • • • • •

# BEEF BURRITO

*You might not immediately think of topping mac n' cheese with lettuce, but the textural contrast makes the combination a winner.* **Serves 5**

1 box deluxe mac n' cheese

1½ cups ground beef

1 tablespoon water

1 teaspoon cumin

1 teaspoon onion powder

1 teaspoon garlic salt

1 teaspoon black pepper

¼ cup finely chopped jalapeño

1 (10-ounce) can refried beans

½ cup sour cream, divided

hot sauce

1 cup shredded lettuce

¼ cup chopped onion

**1.** Cook the mac n' cheese as directed, and set aside.

**2.** In a large nonstick skillet over medium-high heat, brown the ground meat, breaking it into small pieces with a wooden spoon. Cook, stirring occasionally, until browned and cooked through, about 10 minutes. Drain off the fat. Reduce the heat to low, and add the water, cumin, onion powder, garlic salt, and black pepper. Continue to cook, stirring occasionally, for 5 minutes.

**3.** Warm the mac n' cheese over medium heat, and when hot, combine it with the beef, jalapeño, refried beans, and ¼ cup sour cream. Stir well to incorporate. Transfer to serving dishes and top with hot sauce to taste, shredded lettuce, onion, and remaining ¼ cup sour cream.

• • • • • • • • •

# TURKEY CLUB

*The turkey club is one of my favorite sandwiches because of the combination of salty bacon, crispy lettuce, and creamy mayo or sour cream. That same awesome combo is even better with mac n' cheese joining the party.* **Serves 5 or 6**

1 box deluxe mac n' cheese

8 ounces bacon (½ package)

¼ cup sour cream

½ cup Colby Jack cheese (2 ounces)

2 teaspoons black pepper

1½ cups shredded or chopped leftover roast turkey

**1.** Cook the mac n' cheese as directed, and set aside.

**2.** In a large nonstick skillet over medium-high heat, cook the bacon, turning when crisp on the underside, until cooked through and crisp on both sides, 10 to 15 minutes. Remove and drain on paper towels. Once the bacon has cooled, crumble it into small pieces.

**3.** Mix together the mac n' cheese, sour cream, Colby Jack cheese, black pepper, roast turkey, and crumbled bacon.

• • • • • • • • •

# STEAK BURRITO

*When we're grilling steaks, I love grilling an extra steak, taking that one piece, and making an entire meal out of it for the whole family the next day. I always enjoy making any recipe that includes a delicious Mexican queso fresco.* **Serves 5 or 6**

1 box deluxe mac n' cheese

1½ cups chopped leftover grilled steak

1 cup crumbled queso fresco (4 ounces)

1 (10-ounce) can refried beans

1 jalapeño, seeded and chopped

1 medium tomato, seeded and chopped

1 tablespoon chopped fresh cilantro

1 medium avocado, chopped

**1.** Cook the mac n' cheese as directed.

**2.** Add the steak, queso fresco, beans, jalapeño, and tomato, stirring until well mixed. Transfer to a serving dish and top with cilantro and avocado.

• • • • • • • •

# SIMPLE FISH TACOS

*Frozen fish fillets are my go-to when I don't have time to get fresh fish from the market. When I was growing up, my family always ate fish sticks with mac n' cheese and broccoli, so combining mac with fish reminds me of home.* **Serves 1**

1 (19-ounce) package frozen fish fillets

small (6-inch) soft flour or corn tortillas

½ cup leftover cooked mac n' cheese per taco

¼ cup shredded Mexican cheese blend (1 ounce)

1 tablespoon pico de gallo per taco

**1.** Cook the fish fillets as directed. Be sure the fish is cooked through and the outside is golden brown.

**2.** Divide the cooked fish among the tortillas. Layer the mac n' cheese, Mexican cheese, and pico de gallo over the fish in each tortilla. Top with your favorite hot sauce or sour cream.

• • • • • • • • •

# FARMER'S MARKET PIZZA

*When I spent a summer traveling across the country, I developed a love for visiting local farmer's markets. It is fascinating to see how the produce varies from place to place, with each market offering something unique.* **Serves 4 or 5**

1 small zucchini, chopped

1 medium red bell pepper, chopped

1 small red onion, chopped

2 cloves garlic, chopped

2 tablespoons olive oil, plus more for topping

1 teaspoon garlic salt

1 teaspoon black pepper

1 prepared pizza dough

1 cup prepared marinara sauce

1½ cups leftover cooked mac n' cheese

1 cup shredded fresh mozzarella (4 ounces)

7 to 8 large fresh basil leaves

**1.** Preheat the oven to 425°F. Place the zucchini, bell pepper, red onion, and garlic in a large bowl. Drizzle the olive oil over the top, add the garlic salt and black pepper, and toss until the vegetables are well coated. Place the coated vegetables on a nonstick baking sheet, and bake until they start to soften, about 15 minutes.

**2.** In the meantime, roll out the pizza dough. Cover your work surface lightly with flour to prevent the dough from sticking to the surface. Using a rolling pin, roll the dough to the desired thickness. Spread the marinara sauce and then the mac n' cheese over the dough. Once the vegetables are done, remove them from the oven and evenly distribute them over the mac n' cheese. Top with the mozzarella cheese.

**3.** Transfer the pizza to the baking sheet, return to the oven, and cook until the crust has slightly browned and the cheese has started to brown, 5 to 10 minutes. Remove from the oven, and top with fresh basil leaves and an additional drizzle of olive oil.

• • • • • • • • •

# MEATLESS SOUTH-OF-THE-BORDER TACOS

*When I was in college, I was always tempted to order Mexican food since it was quick, convenient, and, of course, tasty. The problem is that being on a strict budget and ordering out don't always go together. I would make this in my dorm room with microwavable mac n' cheese, but you can make it with regular mac on the stove.* **Serves 4 or 5**

1 box mac n' cheese

1 (1-ounce) packet prepared taco seasoning

1 medium tomato, chopped

1 jalapeño, seeded and chopped

*Optional toppings: shredded cheese, sour cream, shredded lettuce*

**1.** Cook the mac n' cheese as directed.

**2.** Add the taco seasoning and stir well to combine. Then stir in the tomato and jalapeño. Top with shredded cheese, a dollop of sour cream, or shredded lettuce.

. . . . . . . . .

# VEGETARIAN

I'm definitely a meat-lover, but you don't have to be a vegetarian to enjoy these meatless options. Whether you just want a break from meat or are trying to save a few dollars by omitting it, you won't be missing it with these recipes.

# SKINNY MAC

*Ever since my husband entered the medical field, we've tried to make healthy choices when possible in recipes. I switch out regular noodles for whole grain and then swap my usual cheese for a reduced-fat variety. It tastes just as great as a meal but has less fat and fewer calories.* **Serves 5**

1 box whole grain mac n' cheese

1 tablespoon olive oil

1 small onion, chopped

1 medium green bell pepper, chopped

1 cup chopped mushrooms

1 cup shredded reduced-fat mozzarella cheese (4 ounces)

**1.** Cook the mac n' cheese as directed, and set aside.

**2.** Heat the olive oil in a large skillet over medium heat. Add the onion, bell pepper, and mushrooms, stirring occasionally, until tender, about 10 minutes. Add the cooked mac n' cheese, mixing until well combined. Then stir in the mozzarella cheese.

* * * * * * * * *

# STUFFED SHELLS

*Every holiday season, my family stuffs large pasta shells with seasoned ricotta cheese and bakes them in homemade marinara sauce. That heavenly dish inspired this recipe, which holds me over until Christmas.* **Serves 5**

1 box shell mac n' cheese

2½ cups prepared marinara sauce

¼ cup grated Parmesan cheese (1 ounce), plus more for topping

½ cup whole milk ricotta cheese (2 ounces)

5 or 6 chopped fresh basil leaves

**1.** Cook the mac n' cheese as directed, and set aside.

**2.** In a medium pot over medium heat, cook the marinara sauce. Add the cooked, still hot mac n' cheese, the Parmesan cheese, ricotta cheese, and basil to the sauce and stir to combine. Top with additional Parmesan cheese.

• • • • • • • • •

# SANTA FE PEPPER PASTA

*The blue corn tortilla chips give the mac n' cheese a satisfying crunch, and their color makes this dish really pop. Poblano peppers are mild chile peppers. Choose green poblanos over red if you're not a fan of heat.* **Serves 5**

1 box mac n' cheese

1 tablespoon olive oil

1 poblano pepper, seeded and chopped

1 clove garlic, finely chopped

1 cup shredded Monterey Jack cheese (4 ounces)

1 cup crumbled blue corn tortilla chips (4 ounces)

**1.** Cook the mac n' cheese as directed, and set aside.

**2.** Heat the olive oil in a large skillet over medium-low heat. Add the poblano pepper and garlic and cook until tender, about 5 minutes. Stir in the cooked mac n' cheese until well combined. Then mix in the Monterey Jack cheese until it has melted. Serve with crumbled tortilla chips on top.

• • • • • • • • •

# SIZZLING FAJITA MAC

*The lime zest gives this dish an even bolder flavor than when just the juice is used. I like pepper jack cheese for a kick, but you could substitute cheddar or a Mexican blend.* **Serves 5 or 6**

1 box mac n' cheese

1 tablespoon olive oil

1 small onion, chopped

1 medium green bell pepper, chopped

zest and juice of 1 lime

1 cup pepper jack cheese (4 ounces)

**1.** Cook the mac n' cheese as directed, and set aside.

**2.** Heat the oil in a large skillet over medium heat. Add the onion and pepper and cook until the vegetables are softened and the onion is translucent, about 10 minutes. Stir in the lime zest and juice, and continue cooking for an additional 3 minutes. Add the cooked mac n' cheese, mixing until well combined. Stir in the pepper jack cheese until it has melted.

* * * * * * * * *

# SPINACH ARTICHOKE MAC

*Spinach artichoke dip always makes its way to get-togethers, so instead of eating it with tortilla chips, the mac n' cheese turns into a hearty meal.* **Serves 5**

1 box deluxe four-cheese mac n' cheese

2 cups chopped jarred, canned, or frozen and thawed, drained artichokes

2 cups cooked fresh or frozen, thawed, and drained spinach

1 cup prepared Alfredo sauce

2 tablespoons chopped roasted red pepper

1 teaspoon garlic salt

1 teaspoon Italian seasoning blend

1 teaspoon dried oregano

1 teaspoon black pepper

2 cups grated Asiago cheese (8 ounces), divided

1 cup grated Parmesan cheese (4 ounces), divided

**1.** Preheat the oven to 400°F. Cook the mac n' cheese as directed.

**2.** While the mac n' cheese is cooking, in a large pot over medium-low heat, combine the artichoke, spinach, Alfredo sauce, roasted red pepper, garlic salt, Italian seasoning, oregano, black pepper, 1 cup Asiago cheese, and ½ cup Parmesan cheese. Cook, stirring occasionally, for about 10 minutes, or the time it takes to cook the mac n' cheese.

**3.** Once the mac n' cheese is prepared, add it to the spinach and artichoke mixture, stirring until well combined. Transfer to a 9 x 13-inch baking dish and top with the remaining 1 cup Asiago cheese and ½ cup Parmesan cheese. Bake uncovered until the cheeses are fully melted and have started to brown, about 20 minutes.

• • • • • • • • •

# CORN CHOWD-A

*You would be hard-pressed to find such a satisfying dish that's easier to make than this one. Although simple and containing only four ingredients, it creates something unexpected with mac n' cheese.* **Serves 5 or 6**

1 box deluxe mac n' cheese

1 (10-ounce) can condensed cream of mushroom soup

½ cup milk

2 cups fresh or frozen corn kernels

**1.** Cook the mac n' cheese as directed.

**2.** While the mac n' cheese is cooking, in a large saucepan over low heat, add the canned soup and milk. Stir to combine and cook for 5 minutes. Stir in the corn and continue to cook until heated through, about 10 minutes. Add the hot, cooked mac n' cheese, and stir until well combined, then remove from the heat. To serve, ladle into bowls.

· · · · · · · · ·

# CREAMY FIESTA MAC

*In my college dorm, when I didn't have access to a stove, I would make microwavable mac n' cheese and simply mix in a scoop of cream cheese and a scoop of salsa. It's creamy, tasty, and super easy.* **Serves 4 or 5**

1 box mac n' cheese                1 cup cream cheese

1 cup prepared salsa

**1.** Cook the mac n' cheese as directed. While it's hot, add the cream cheese and stir until well blended. Add the salsa and continue to stir until well incorporated.

• • • • • • • •

# MEDITERRANEAN MAC

*When Chicago weather permits, I love cooking vegetables outdoors on my charcoal grill. Grilled or roasted vegetables have such robust flavor that adding them to mac n' cheese really elevates the dish.*

**Serves 4 or 5**

1 box mac n' cheese

1 medium onion, chopped

1 large zucchini, chopped

1 medium red bell pepper, chopped

1 tablespoon olive oil

1 teaspoon garlic salt

1 teaspoon black pepper

1 teaspoon Italian seasoning blend

¼ cup sun-dried tomatoes

1 cup Italian cheese blend (4 ounces)

**1.** Cook the mac n' cheese as directed, and set aside.

**2.** Place the onion, zucchini, and bell pepper in a large bowl, and drizzle on the olive oil. Add the garlic salt, black pepper, and Italian seasoning, and toss until the vegetables are well coated.

**3.** If grilling the vegetables outdoors on a gas or charcoal grill, cook until the vegetables begin to soften. If you don't have access to a grill, cook the vegetables in an oven preheated to 425°F. Arrange in a single layer on a nonstick baking sheet and bake for 15 to 20 minutes.

**4.** Add the roasted vegetables to the pot with the mac n' cheese and stir to combine. Add the sun-dried tomatoes and Italian cheese blend, stirring until well combined.

• • • • • • • •

# AMORE MAC

*Noodles and red sauce—it's a classic duo. The dish is simple to make, and you can use any kind of homemade or store-bought tomato-based sauce. Many jarred sauces contain good ingredients and come in varieties such as roasted red pepper or spicy garlic.* **Serves 4 or 5**

1 box deluxe four-cheese mac n' cheese

1½ cups prepared marinara sauce

1½ cups shredded mozzarella cheese (6 ounces)

½ cup grated Parmesan or Romano cheese (2 ounces)

**1.** Cook the mac n' cheese as directed. Meanwhile, heat the marinara sauce in a small saucepan over medium-low heat or in the microwave.

**2.** Add the heated sauce to the cooked mac n' cheese and stir to combine. Stir in the mozzarella cheese and the Parmesan or Romano cheese until well incorporated.

· · · · · · · · ·

# MEATLESS GREEK

*Fresh spinach sautéed in olive oil and garlic is one of my favorite foods. However, I do keep frozen spinach on hand for times when I don't have fresh but still want to throw it into a dish.* **Serves 4 or 5**

1 box mac n' cheese

1½ cups crumbled feta cheese (6 ounces)

2 cups cooked fresh spinach or thawed frozen spinach

1 teaspoon garlic salt

1 teaspoon black pepper

**1.** Cook the mac n' cheese as directed. While it is hot, combine it with the feta cheese, spinach, garlic salt, and black pepper. Stir until well blended.

• • • • • • • •

# VEGETARIAN'S FIESTA

*I enjoy transforming a dish I usually make with meat into completely vegetarian fare. I love meat, but going meatless is a nice change, not to mention a great way to save some time and money.* **Serves 4 or 5**

1 box mac n' cheese

1 teaspoon cumin

1 teaspoon garlic salt

1 teaspoon black pepper

1 teaspoon cayenne pepper

1 teaspoon onion powder

1 medium tomato, chopped

½ medium onion, chopped

1 jalapeño, seeded and chopped

½ cup fresh cilantro

1 cup crumbled tortilla chips (about 1 ounce)

*Optional toppings: sour cream, guacamole*

**1.** Cook the mac n' cheese as directed.

**2.** While the cooked mac n' cheese is hot, add the cumin, garlic salt, black pepper, cayenne pepper, onion powder, tomato, onion, jalapeño, and cilantro, stirring until well combined. Top with crumbled tortilla chips, and sour cream or guacamole.

· · · · · · · · ·

# PASTA PRIMAVERA

*My family is Italian-American, but my older sister is a vegetarian so adding vegetables instead of a meat-laden tomato sauce to pasta is a common switch that I've grown to love.* **Serves 4 or 5**

1 box mac n' cheese

2 tablespoons olive oil

1 clove garlic, finely chopped

1 small zucchini, chopped

1 medium red bell pepper, chopped

1 cup chopped fresh, canned, or frozen and thawed Italian-style green beans

1 teaspoon Italian seasoning blend

½ teaspoon dried oregano

1 teaspoon black pepper

2 teaspoons garlic salt

1 cup grated Parmesan cheese (4 ounces)

**1.** Cook the mac n' cheese as directed.

**2.** While the mac n' cheese is cooking, heat the olive oil in a large skillet over medium heat. Add the garlic, zucchini, bell pepper, green beans, Italian seasoning, oregano, black pepper, and garlic salt. Cook, stirring occasionally, until the vegetables start to soften, 5 to 10 minutes.

**3.** Add the vegetable mixture and Parmesan cheese to the hot mac n' cheese. Stir until well blended.

· · · · · · · · ·

# GREEN BEAN MAC

*Thanksgiving dinner isn't the only occasion for a green bean casserole. Mac n' cheese turns this traditional fare into something special for a complete meal or a side dish.* **Serves 4 or 5**

1 box mac n' cheese

2 cups chopped fresh, canned, or frozen and thawed green beans

1 (10-ounce) can cream of mushroom soup

½ cup grated Parmesan cheese (2 ounces)

1 teaspoon black pepper

2 cups crispy onion straws

**1.** Cook the mac n' cheese as directed.

**2.** Turn the heat to low, and to the pot containing the cooked mac n' cheese, add the green beans, canned soup, Parmesan cheese, and black pepper. Stir to combine. Heat through, about 10 minutes. Top with crispy onion straws.

• • • • • • • •

# THAI MAC

*In this recipe the peanuts and shredded carrots add crunch, and the cilantro a burst of freshness—and they all work deliciously with mac n' cheese.* **Serves 4 or 5**

1 box mac n' cheese

½ cup chopped red bell pepper

½ cup chopped scallions

2 tablespoons Thai chile sauce

1 cup shredded carrots

½ cup fresh cilantro

2 cups unsalted roasted peanuts

**1.** Cook the mac n' cheese as directed, and set aside.

**2.** When the mac n' cheese has cooled, transfer it to a large bowl. Add the bell pepper, scallions, and Thai chile sauce, and stir until well blended. Top with the shredded carrot, cilantro, and peanuts.

• • • • • • • • •

# THE OLD WEST

*The West is my favorite part of the country. When I traveled there, I was expecting to enjoy the new scenery, but I was pleasantly surprised by the unique foods from the region. I love the influence from the southern states as well as from Mexico. I enjoy the distinct flavor of blue corn tortilla chips in this dish.* **Serves 4 or 5**

1 box deluxe sharp cheddar mac n' cheese

1 (16-ounce) package Southwest blend frozen vegetables or 2 cups mixed corn, chopped green bell pepper, and chopped red bell pepper

1 teaspoon garlic salt

2 teaspoons black pepper

2 cups shredded pepper jack cheese (8 ounces), divided

1 cup crumbled blue corn tortilla chips (4 ounces)

**1.** Preheat the oven to 425°F. Cook the mac n' cheese as directed.

**2.** Add the vegetables, garlic salt, black pepper, and 1 cup pepper jack cheese to the cooked mac n' cheese. Transfer to a 9 x 13-inch baking dish, and top with the remaining 1 cup pepper jack cheese. Bake uncovered until the cheese is melted and starts to brown, at least 10 minutes. Remove from the oven and top with the crumbled tortilla chips.

• • • • • • • • •

# POULTRY & FISH

Chicken is such a staple in our diets, and sometimes we end up making the same dishes with it. But these mac n' cheese recipes combine the chicken with the familiar flavors of mac along with other ingredients to create something more interesting, like Italian Mac (page 84), where pesto adds a fresh pop of flavor. Growing up, my family would often have fish sticks with our mac n' cheese, so for me fish and mac are a natural pair.

# CHICKEN PARM MAC

*Topping mac n' cheese with a layer of two different cheeses and bread crumbs gives this dish that scrumptious chicken Parmesan taste without the time it takes to fry the chicken. For an extra crunch, use seasoned panko bread crumbs instead of the classic Italian-style.* **Serves 5**

1 box deluxe four-cheese mac n' cheese

2½ cups marinara sauce

2 cups shredded leftover cooked chicken

1 cup shredded mozzarella cheese (8 ounces), divided

1 cup grated Parmesan cheese (8 ounces), divided

½ cup Italian-style bread crumbs

**1.** Preheat the oven to 425°F. Cook the mac n' cheese as directed, and set aside.

**2.** Heat the marinara sauce in a large pot over medium heat, about 5 minutes. Add the chicken, ½ cup mozzarella cheese, ½ cup Parmesan cheese, and the cooked mac n' cheese. Stir to combine, and cook for another 5 minutes, until heated through. Transfer to a 9 x 13-inch baking dish.

**3.** Mix the remaining ½ cup mozzarella cheese and ½ cup Parmesan cheese with the bread crumbs. Evenly distribute over the mac n' cheese mixture in the baking dish. Bake uncovered until the top starts to brown, 5 to 10 minutes.

• • • • • • • • •

# MAMA MIA MAC

*Rich Alfredo sauce makes this 'mac n' cheese the ultimate comfort food. I often order broccoli alfredo pasta when out to dinner, and this recipe is a quick way to re-create the restaurant-quality meal.*

**Serves 5 or 6**

1 box deluxe four-cheese mac n' cheese

2 cups cooked broccoli florets

2 cups shredded leftover cooked chicken

1 cup prepared Alfredo sauce

1½ cups Italian cheese blend (6 ounces)

**1.** Cook the mac n' cheese as directed.

**2.** While the cooked mac n' cheese is still hot, add the broccoli, chicken, Alfredo sauce, and Italian cheese blend. Stir until well incorporated and the cheese has melted.

\* \* \* \* \* \* \* \*

# MAC AU VIN

*I love the idea of combining the refined French dish coq au vin with an out-of-the-box ingredient. For this recipe, I swap out my usual white meat chicken for richer dark meat.* **Serves 3 or 4**

1 box deluxe mac n' cheese

1 tablespoon butter

1 large onion, chopped

1 large carrot, chopped

1 rib celery, chopped

4 cloves garlic, finely chopped

½ cup sliced mushrooms

1 bay leaf

1 teaspoon garlic salt

1 teaspoon dried thyme

1 teaspoon black pepper

1 (15-ounce) can tomato sauce

1½ cups leftover cooked dark meat chicken

**1.** Cook the mac n' cheese as directed, and set aside.

**2.** In a large pot over medium heat, start melting the butter and add the onion, carrot, celery, and garlic. Cook, stirring occasionally, for 5 minutes. Add the mushrooms, bay leaf, garlic salt, thyme, black pepper, and tomato sauce. Cook, stirring occasionally, for an additional 10 minutes.

**3.** Stir in the chicken, and turn the heat to low. Cook for another 5 minutes, then remove the bay leaf. Add the mac n' cheese, stirring well to incorporate.

• • • • • • • • •

# COWBOY'S MAC

*Every time I make this mac n' cheese, I use a different flavor barbecue sauce—for example, chipotle honey or sweet and spicy—to revamp the dish.* **Serves 4 or 5**

1 box mac n' cheese

2 cups shredded leftover cooked chicken

¼ cup shredded pepper jack cheese (1 ounce)

¼ cup shredded sharp cheddar cheese (1 ounce)

1 teaspoon hot sauce

1½ cups barbecue sauce of choice

1½ cups crispy onion straws

**1.** Cook the mac n' cheese as directed.

**2.** Add the chicken, pepper jack cheese, cheddar cheese, and hot sauce to the mac n' cheese, and stir until well combined. Add the barbecue sauce and stir until the chicken and noodles are well coated. Top with crispy onion straws.

* * * * * * * * *

# ITALIAN MAC

*Whether it's homemade or store-bought, pesto adds a fresh pop to this mac n' cheese dish. The bread crumbs make a crispy coating that everyone will love.* **Serves 4 or 5**

1 box deluxe four-cheese mac n' cheese

1 cup grated Asiago cheese (4 ounces), divided

2 cup shredded leftover cooked chicken

¼ cup pesto

1 teaspoon garlic salt

2 teaspoons Italian seasoning blend

½ cup Italian-style bread crumbs

**1.** Preheat the oven to 425°F. Cook the mac n' cheese as directed.

**2.** Add ½ cup Asiago cheese along with the chicken, pesto, garlic salt, and Italian seasoning to the cooked mac n' cheese. Mix until well blended. Transfer to a 9 x 13-inch baking dish. Top with the bread crumbs and remaining ½ cup Asiago cheese. Bake uncovered until the cheese starts to melt and the bread crumbs are browned, about 15 minutes.

• • • • • • • • •

# CHICKEN ENCHILADA MAC

*In this recipe, I use either white or dark meat chicken, or both, shredded and smothered in enchilada sauce and partnered with vegetables. Then, instead of wrapping everything in corn tortillas, I depart from tradition by using mac n' cheese to bring the meal together.* **Serves 4 or 5**

1 box deluxe mac n' cheese

2 tablespoons olive oil

⅓ cup chopped onion

½ cup chopped green bell pepper

1 jalapeño, seeded and chopped

⅛ teaspoon cumin

⅛ teaspoon cayenne pepper

1 cup shredded leftover cooked chicken

1 (10-ounce) can enchilada sauce

½ cup Mexican cheese blend (2 ounces)

**1.** Cook the mac n' cheese as directed, and set aside.

**2.** Heat the olive oil in a large deep skillet over medium heat. Add the onion, bell pepper, jalapeño, cumin, and cayenne pepper. Cook, stirring occasionally, until the vegetables are tender and the onion is translucent, about 10 minutes.

**3.** Add the chicken, enchilada sauce, Mexican cheese, and cooked mac n' cheese to the vegetable mixture. Stir until well blended.

• • • • • • • • •

# CHICKEN PICCATA

*Using both the zest and juice of a lemon makes this dish taste super fresh and gives it a tangy flavor. The capers add even more tartness, while the creamy mac n' cheese tones it down and brings it all together.* **Serves 4 or 5**

1 box deluxe four-cheese mac n' cheese

1 cup prepared Alfredo sauce

zest of 1 medium lemon

juice of ½ medium lemon

2 teaspoons capers

⅛ teaspoon black pepper

½ cup grated Parmesan cheese (2 ounces)

2 cups shredded or chopped leftover cooked chicken

**1.** Cook the mac n' cheese as directed, and set aside.

**2.** Heat the Alfredo sauce in a medium saucepan over low heat. Stir in the lemon zest, lemon juice, capers, black pepper, and Parmesan cheese. Cook, stirring occasionally, for 5 minutes. Add the sauce and chicken to the mac n' cheese, and stir until well blended.

• • • • • • • • •

# THANKSGIVING WITH A TWIST

*There are only so many turkey sandwiches I can eat after Thanksgiving. To get through all the leftovers, I switch it up by combining turkey with mac n' cheese.* **Serves 4 or 5**

1 box mac n' cheese

½ cup cranberry sauce

¼ cup sliced Brie cheese

½ cup shredded leftover cooked turkey

**1.** Cook the mac n' cheese as directed, and set aside.

**2.** While the mac is cooking, heat the cranberry sauce in a medium saucepan over low heat. Add the Brie cheese and continue cooking, stirring occasionally, until the Brie has melted into the sauce, 5 to 10 minutes. Add the turkey and the cranberry and Brie sauce to the hot mac n' cheese, and stir until well blended.

• • • • • • • • •

# SUPERBOWL MAC

*Buffalo wings are always a favorite party food, but they can be really messy to handle. I use mac n' cheese to make my interpretation of buffalo wings more filling and easier to eat.* **Serves 5**

1 box mac n' cheese

1½ cups shredded leftover cooked chicken

½ cup chopped celery

½ cup crumbled Gorgonzola cheese (2 ounces)

1 cup prepared buffalo sauce

**1.** Cook the mac n' cheese as directed.

**2.** Add the chicken, celery, Gorgonzola cheese, and buffalo sauce to the cooked mac n' cheese. Stir until well blended.

• • • • • • • • •

# BARBECUE CHICKEN MAC

*When I lived in college dorms, I would get bored with cafeteria food. Instead of ordering out, I would use cooked chicken leftover from the night before and add it along with barbecue sauce to mac n' cheese.* **Serves 4 or 5**

1 box mac n' cheese

2 cups shredded leftover cooked chicken

1 cup prepared barbecue sauce

**1.** Cook the mac n' cheese as directed.

**2.** Mix the shredded chicken into the cooked mac n' cheese. Then add the barbecue sauce, stirring until the sauce completely coats the chicken and noodles.

● ● ● ● ● ● ● ● ●

# SOUTHERN FRIED CHICKEN

*Turn leftover fried chicken into an entirely different meal by adding it to mac n' cheese. A touch of creamy ranch dressing completes the dish.* **Serves 4 or 5**

1 box mac n' cheese

1 cup shredded leftover fried chicken

½ cup prepared creamy ranch dressing

**1.** Cook the mac n' cheese as directed.

**2.** Add the chicken and ranch dressing to the cooked mac n' cheese, stirring until well blended.

. . . . . . . . .

# NOT YOUR GRANDMA'S TUNA CASSEROLE

*Combining a classic homemade dish like tuna casserole with a convenience food like boxed mac n' cheese gives this traditional family meal an easy makeover.* **Serves 5 or 6**

1 box deluxe mac n' cheese

1 tablespoon butter

1 medium onion, chopped

1 cup chopped green bell pepper

1 bay leaf

1 (10-ounce) can cream of mushroom soup

1 (5-ounce) can tuna, drained

½ cup shredded Colby Jack cheese (4 ounces)

¼ cup bread crumbs

**1.** Preheat the oven to 425°F. Cook the mac n' cheese as directed.

**2.** While the mac n' cheese is cooking, in a large skillet over medium-low heat, start melting the butter. Add the onion, bell pepper, and bay leaf. Cook, stirring occasionally, until the vegetables are tender and the onion is translucent, about 10 minutes.

**3.** Stir in the canned soup. Turn the heat down to low and cook for an additional 5 minutes. Stir in the tuna and cook for another 3 to 5 minutes. Add the cooked mac n' cheese to the mixture and stir to combine.

**4.** Transfer to a 9 x 13-inch baking dish. Evenly distribute the Colby Jack cheese and bread crumbs over the top. Bake uncovered until the top starts to brown, 25 minutes.

• • • • • • • • •

# EAST COAST MAC

*During a road trip on the East Coast, I fell in love with the scenery and the food. This play on clam chowder featuring mac n' cheese captures my admiration for the region.* **Serves 5 or 6**

1 box deluxe mac n' cheese

1 tablespoon butter

1 medium yellow onion, chopped

1 medium carrot, chopped

1 rib celery, chopped

⅛ teaspoon Old Bay Seasoning

⅛ teaspoon salt

1 cup canned clams

½ cup heavy cream

1 (15-ounce) can cream of potato soup

2 cups oyster crackers

**1.** Cook the mac n' cheese as directed, and set aside.

**2.** In a large pot over medium-low heat, start melting the butter and then add the onion, carrot, celery, Old Bay Seasoning, and salt. Cook, stirring occasionally, for 10 minutes or until the vegetables begin to soften and the onion is translucent.

**3.** Stir in the clams, heavy cream, and canned soup, and cook for an additional 10 minutes. Add the cooked mac n' cheese, stirring until well mixed. Ladle into serving bowls and top with oyster crackers.

• • • • • • • • •

# SHRIMP BROCCOLI ALFREDO

*Whenever frozen shrimp is on sale, I buy it to add to mac n' cheese to give the mac a refined twist. Alfredo sauce lends a rich flavor, and Parmesan cheese imparts a delightful, nutty taste.* **Serves 5 or 6**

1 box deluxe four-cheese mac n' cheese

1½ cups broccoli florets

1½ cups prepared Alfredo sauce

1 teaspoon Italian seasoning blend

1 cup frozen and thawed, chopped, cooked shrimp

½ cup Parmesan cheese (4 ounces)

**1.** Cook the mac n' cheese as directed.

**2.** While the mac n' cheese is cooking, steam the broccoli until tender, about 10 minutes.

**3.** In a large skillet over medium heat, cook the Alfredo sauce, stirring occasionally, until heated through, about 5 minutes. Add the cooked broccoli and Italian seasoning, and cook for an additional 5 minutes. Then stir in the shrimp and cook until heated through, 8 to 10 minutes.

**4.** Add the Parmesan cheese and cooked mac n' cheese to the sauce containing the broccoli and shrimp. Stir until well combined.

· · · · · · · · ·

# PORK

Adding pork, such as Italian sausage, marinated pork chops, or bratwurst, gives these mac n' cheese meals a punch of flavor. The recipes loaded with bacon, like the Bacon Lover's Mac, add a smoked, savory element that transforms the boxed mac n' cheese into something decadent.

# OKTOBERFEST CASSEROLE

*Classic German ingredients work fantastically well with sharp cheddar mac n' cheese. To get the Oktoberfest feeling, I love to wash this dish down with a crisp wheat beer.* **Serves 6**

1 box deluxe sharp cheddar mac n' cheese

2 tablespoons olive oil

4 tablespoons butter, divided

1 large onion, thinly sliced

2 smoked bratwurst links, chopped

1 tablespoon spicy brown mustard

½ cup ground pretzels (grind in food processor or blender)

¼ cup shredded sharp cheddar cheese (2 ounces)

**1.** Cook the mac n' cheese as directed, and set aside.

**2.** Heat the olive oil and 2 tablespoons butter in a large skillet over medium-low heat. Cook the onion, stirring occasionally, until translucent, 15 to 20 minutes. Turn the heat to low and add the chopped bratwurst and cook, stirring occasionally, for an additional 5 minutes.

**3.** Preheat the oven's broiler to low. Add the cooked mac n' cheese and mustard to the onion and bratwurst mixture, stirring until well mixed. Transfer to a 9 x 13-inch baking dish.

**4.** Melt 2 tablespoons butter in a small saucepan over medium-low heat. In a small bowl, mix the ground pretzels with the melted butter. Evenly distribute the cheddar cheese and then the pretzel mixture on the top of the casserole. Broil until the cheese has melted and the pretzel topping starts to brown, 3 to 6 minutes.

• • • • • • • • •

# JERSEY MAC N' SAUSAGE

*Once I really started to get serious about cooking, I discovered many types of sausage. For a twist, I like to use sausage with different ingredients in it like sweet roasted red pepper or cheese. For a healthier option, try Italian turkey sausage.* **Serves 6**

1 box deluxe mac n' cheese

8 ounces mild or spicy Italian sausage (about 3 links)

1 medium green bell pepper, chopped

2½ cups marinara sauce

1 cup Italian cheese blend (4 ounces)

**1.** Cook the mac n' cheese as directed, and set aside.

**2.** In a medium nonstick skillet over medium heat, cook the sausage, breaking it into small pieces with a rubber spatula, until browned and cooked through, 10 minutes. Add the bell pepper and cook, stirring occasionally, until softened, about 5 minutes.

**3.** Turn the heat to low. Stir in the marinara sauce and cook for an additional 5 to 10 minutes. Add the cooked mac n' cheese and cheese, stirring until well incorporated, and cook until the cheese is melted, about 5 minutes.

• • • • • • • • •

# NEW ORLEANS CAJUN

*This recipe needs Cajun spices for authentic flavor. Look in the spice aisle for a premade Cajun seasoning blend. If you can't find one, simply combine about 1 teaspoon each of paprika, garlic powder, onion powder, black pepper, and cayenne pepper for a similar taste.* **Serves 5**

1 box shell mac n' cheese

2 tablespoons olive oil

5 ounces andouille sausage (about 1 link), casing removed

1 small onion, chopped

½ medium green bell pepper, chopped

½ medium red bell pepper, chopped

2 cloves garlic, minced

1 teaspoon Cajun seasoning blend

**1.** Cook the mac n' cheese as directed, and set aside.

**2.** Heat the olive oil in a large skillet over medium-low heat. Add the sausage and cook until browned and cooked through, about 10 minutes. As the sausage cooks, break it up into small pieces with a rubber spatula.

**3.** Add the onion and bell peppers to the sausage and cook, stirring occasionally, until the vegetables are softened and the onion is translucent, about 10 minutes. Stir in the garlic and Cajun seasoning, and cook another 2 minutes. Add the cooked, hot mac n' cheese, stirring until well mixed.

• • • • • • • • •

# BACON LOVER'S MAC

*Sometimes I'm inspired by culinary excellence, and sometimes I'm not. In this case, it is bacon lover Homer Simpson who inspired this indulgent bacon-filled recipe.* **Serves 5**

1 box mac n' cheese

6 slices thick-cut bacon, sliced thick

2 slices Canadian bacon

6 ounces sliced pancetta

**1.** Cook the mac n' cheese as directed.

**2.** While the mac n' cheese is cooking, cook the two types of bacon and the pancetta in a large nonstick skillet over medium-high heat. Turn the bacon and pancetta when crisp on the underside, until cooked through and crisp on both sides, 10 to 15 minutes. Remove and drain on paper towels. Once the meats have cooled, crumble into small pieces.

**3.** Stir the cooked meats into the cooked mac n' cheese until well mixed.

· · · · · · · · ·

# CAROLINA PULLED PORK

*Every time I make pulled pork in my crock pot, I always end up with leftovers. Instead of using it just in sandwiches, mixing it with mac n' cheese turns it into an entirely different dish. You can also find prepared pulled pork at your grocery store.* **Serves 6**

1 box mac n' cheese

2 cups leftover pulled pork

½ cup chopped scallions

½ cup shredded sharp cheddar cheese (2 ounces)

**1.** Cook the mac n' cheese as directed.

**2.** Heat the leftover pulled pork in a medium pan over medium heat until heated through.

**3.** Add the pulled pork, scallions, and cheddar cheese to the cooked mac n' cheese. Stir until well mixed and the cheese has melted.

• • • • • • • • •

# JALAPEÑO BACON MAC

*Any time I add bacon to a dish, it instantly makes it feel decadent. Bacon and jalapeño always go well together, and the Alfredo sauce adds a silky richness that you might not expect.* **Serves 6**

1 box deluxe mac n' cheese

1 pound bacon (1 package)

½ cup seeded and chopped jalapeño

½ cup prepared Alfredo sauce

½ cup shredded Monterey Jack cheese (2 ounces)

**1.** Cook the mac n' cheese as directed, and set aside.

**2.** In a large nonstick skillet over medium-high heat begin cooking the bacon, turning when not quite crisp on the underside, and continue cooking until nearly done on the other side, 8 to 10 minutes. Remove and drain on paper towels. Remove any excess grease from the pan.

**3.** Place the chopped jalapeño in the skillet. Chop the partially cooked bacon and add back to the skillet. Cook, stirring occasionally, until the bacon is crisp and the jalapeño tender, 7 to 9 minutes.

**4.** In a small saucepan over medium-low heat, warm the Alfredo sauce until heated through.

**5.** Add the bacon, jalapeño, Alfredo sauce, and Monterey Jack cheese to the cooked mac n' cheese. Stir until well mixed.

• • • • • • • • •

# SOUTH BEACH MAC

*A play on the Cuban sandwich—a classic made with ham, roasted pork, Swiss cheese, pickles, and mustard on Cuban bread—this mac n' cheese dish captures all the flavor Miami has to offer.* **Serves 4 or 5**

1 box deluxe mac n' cheese

8 ounces shredded leftover cooked roast pork

8 ounces chopped smoked ham

2 cups Swiss cheese (8 ounces), divided

4 dill pickle slices, chopped

1 tablespoon yellow mustard

**1.** Preheat the oven to 425°F. Cook the mac n' cheese as directed.

**2.** Add the roast pork, smoked ham, and 1 cup Swiss cheese, stirring until well mixed. Transfer to a 9 x 13-inch baking dish and top with the remaining 1 cup Swiss cheese. Bake uncovered until the cheese starts to brown.

**3.** Remove from the oven. Distribute the chopped pickles and drizzle yellow mustard over top.

• • • • • • • • •

# CHINESE TAKE-IN

*My first job was at a Chinese restaurant, where I began to develop a love for the ingredients and flavors. The smell of barbecue pork being made at the restaurant was always guaranteed to make me hungry, and this recipe does the same.* **Serves 5 or 6**

1 box mac n' cheese

8 ounces pork chops, about ½ inch thick (about 3 small)

pinch of salt

¼ teaspoon ground ginger

2 tablespoons prepared barbecue sauce

2 tablespoons olive oil

½ medium head green cabbage, very thinly sliced

2 tablespoons teriyaki sauce

1½ teaspoons Sriracha hot sauce

1 tablespoon soy sauce

1 cup crunchy chow mein noodles

**1.** Cook the mac n' cheese as directed, and set aside.

**2.** Season the pork chops with the salt and ground ginger. In a large nonstick skillet over medium heat, cook the chops until fully cooked inside, turning once, 10 to 15 minutes. Turn the heat to low and smother the chops with the barbecue sauce.

**3.** Heat the olive oil in a clean large skillet over medium-low heat. Add the cabbage, teriyaki sauce, Sriracha, and soy sauce, and cook, stirring occasionally, 10 to 15 minutes. Don't overcook—be sure the cabbage still has some bite to it.

**4.** Add the pork chops and cabbage mixture to the mac n' cheese, and stir well. Top with the crunchy chow mein noodles.

• • • • • • • • •

# CARIBBEAN ISLAND DELIGHT

*A bit spicy, a bit tangy, and a bit fruity, this dish derives its symphony of flavors from the jerk seasonings. My husband and I are always increasing the heat level in dishes and adding more flavors, but this seasoning is so bold, it's great the way it is.* **Serves 5**

8 ounces pork chops, about ½ inch thick (about 3 small)

2 cups prepared jerk seasoning marinade

1 box mac n' cheese

½ cup shredded pepper jack cheese (2 ounces)

**1.** Place the pork chops in a large zip-top storage bag and add the jerk seasoning marinade. Marinate for at least 1 hour in the refrigerator.

**2.** In a large nonstick skillet over medium heat, cook the pork chops until fully cooked inside, turning once, about 5 minutes. Chop into bite-size pieces.

**3.** While the pork is cooking, cook the mac n' cheese as directed. Then add the cooked pork chops and pepper jack cheese.

• • • • • • • • •

# HAM AND CHEESE MAC

*Whether I have leftover ham from a big ham dinner or just some extra lunch meat, I love cutting it up and mixing it with Swiss cheese to create a whole new ham and cheese dish.*  **Serves 5**

1 box mac n' cheese

2 cups shredded Swiss cheese

2 cups diced leftover cooked ham

**1.** Cook the mac n' cheese as directed.

**2.** Add the Swiss cheese and ham, stirring until well mixed.

· · · · · · · · ·

# ALOHA MAC

*Hawaiian pizza was the inspiration for this festive mac n' cheese. Either fresh or canned pineapple gives the mac an unconventional makeover.* **Serves 5 or 6**

1 box mac n' cheese

1 tablespoon butter

1 medium onion, chopped

1 cup diced leftover cooked ham

1 cup chopped pineapple

**1.** Cook the mac n' cheese as directed, and set aside.

**2.** In a large skillet over medium-low heat, start melting the butter. Add the onion and cook, stirring occasionally, until softened, about 15 minutes. Add the ham and pineapple and cook, stirring occasionally, for an additional 5 minutes.

**3.** Add the ham and pineapple mixture to the cooked mac n' cheese. Stir until well blended.

• • • • • • • • •

# RED BEANS AND MAC

*In this recipe I sauté the peppers and onions in the same skillet in which I cooked the bacon to give the entire dish a smoky, meaty flavor.* **Serves 5 or 6**

1 pound bacon (1 package)

1 medium onion, chopped

½ cup green bell pepper

½ cup red bell pepper

1 box mac n' cheese

1 (15-ounce) can kidney beans, drained and rinsed

1 cup diced leftover cooked ham

**1.** In a large deep nonstick skillet over medium-high heat, cook the bacon, turning when crisp on the underside, until cooked through and crisp on both sides, 10 to 12 minutes. Remove and drain on paper towels. Drain all but 1 tablespoon excess oil from the skillet.

**2.** Turn the heat to medium-low and add the onion and bell peppers. Cook, stirring occasionally, until the vegetables are softened and the onion is translucent, about 10 minutes.

**3.** While the onion and peppers are cooking, cook the mac n' cheese as directed.

**4.** Add the beans and ham to the vegetable mixture and continue to cook, stirring occasionally, for an additional 10 minutes. Crumble the cooled bacon and add it to the skillet.

**5.** When both the mac n' cheese and the bean mixture are done, stir the mac n' cheese into the skillet until well blended.

• • • • • • • • •

# CARBONARA MAC

*Growing up, whenever my family made homemade tomato sauce, or "gravy," as it's known to some, it was a treat. But what was fun as I got older and developed a passion for cooking was making something unique out of that leftover sauce. It's amazing how incorporating bacon with spicy crushed red pepper flakes completely alters basic marinara sauce, whether it is leftover or store-bought.* **Serves 4 or 5**

1 pound bacon (1 package)

½ medium onion, chopped

3 cloves garlic, finely chopped

1 tablespoon crushed red pepper flakes

1½ cups prepared marinara sauce

1 box mac n' cheese

½ cup grated Parmesan cheese (2 ounces)

**1.** In a large deep nonstick skillet over medium-high heat, cook the bacon, turning when crisp on the underside, until cooked through and crisp on both sides, 10 to 12 minutes. Remove and drain on paper towels. Drain all but 1 tablespoon excess oil from the skillet. Once the bacon has cooled, cut it into bite-size pieces.

**2.** Turn the heat to medium-low. Add the onion, garlic, and red pepper flakes and cook, stirring occasionally, until the onion is translucent, about 5 minutes. Add the marinara sauce to the onion mixture and cook, stirring occasionally, for an additional 10 minutes. Add the bacon pieces back to the sauce.

**3.** While the sauce is cooking, cook the mac n' cheese as directed.

**4.** Pour the sauce over the mac n' cheese and stir well. Top with the Parmesan cheese.

· · · · · · · · ·

# B-L-T-M

*This dish has such a variety of textures—creamy mac n' cheese and sour cream, crispy bacon, and crunchy lettuce—that it makes a hearty but refreshing meal.* **Serves 5 or 6**

1 pound bacon (1 package)

1 box mac n' cheese

½ cup sour cream

1½ cups shredded iceberg lettuce

**1.** In a large nonstick skillet over medium-high heat, cook the bacon, turning when crisp on the underside, until cooked through and crisp on both sides, 10 to 12 minutes. Remove and drain on paper towels. Once the bacon has cooled, crumble it.

**2.** While the bacon is cooking, prepare the mac n' cheese as directed.

**3.** Add the crumbled bacon and sour cream to the cooked mac n' cheese and stir until well mixed. Top with lettuce.

* * * * * * * *

# ALL-AMERICAN MAC

*At college I often made this mac n' cheese in a microwave when I didn't have access to a stove—but you can make it on a stove if you'd like. It's quick, easy, and a nice break from fast food.* **Serves 4 or 5**

1 box mac n' cheese

3 slices American cheese, chopped

1 cup prepared barbecue sauce

½ cup bacon bits

1 cup crispy onion straws

**1.** Cook the mac n' cheese as directed.

**2.** While the mac n' cheese is still hot, stir in the American cheese, barbecue sauce, and bacon bits. You may need to pop the mixture into the microwave or heat it on the stove to melt the cheese. Once the cheese has melted and everything is well blended, sprinkle the onion straws on top.

* * * * * * * *

# ANTIPASTO MAC

*There are times when I would rather stick to eating appetizers and finger foods rather than a whole meal, and this mac n' cheese dish gives me the best of both worlds.* **Serves 5 or 6**

1 box mac n' cheese

½ cup chopped roasted red pepper

1 cup grated Asiago cheese (4 ounces)

1 cup diced salami

**1.** Cook the mac n' cheese as directed, and set aside.

**2.** Add the roasted red pepper, Asiago cheese, and salami to the cooked mac n' cheese, stirring until well mixed.

● ● ● ● ● ● ● ●

# MAC "SKINS"

*This mac n' cheese recipe turns a fun snack into a filling meal that tastes just like a potato skin loaded with cheese, crispy bacon, and creamy sour cream. When I don't have any scallions on hand, I use dried chives, which I always have in my pantry.* **Serves 4**

2 large russet potatoes

1 cup leftover cooked mac n' cheese

4 tablespoons bacon crumbles

4 tablespoons sour cream

2 tablespoons chopped scallions

1½ cups shredded cheddar cheese (4 ounces), divided

**1.** Preheat the oven to 425°F. Clean the potatoes and poke holes in them with a fork. Place them on an ungreased baking sheet, and bake for 30 minutes. Turn the potatoes and continue baking for an additional 30 minutes. The potatoes are done with they are soft, but they will be very hot so test them with a fork first. Remove from the oven and place on a cooling rack.

**2.** While the potatoes are baking, combine the leftover mac n' cheese, bacon crumbles, sour cream, scallions, and ¼ cup cheddar cheese in a medium bowl. Mix together well, and set aside.

**3.** When the potatoes are cool enough to touch, make a diamond-shaped incision in each. With a small spoon, scoop out the inside of each potato. You can leave as much or as little flesh as you'd like. Save the potato filling for another use. Scoop the mac n' cheese mixture into the potatoes and top with the remaining 1¼ cups cheddar cheese. Return to the oven just long enough to melt the cheese, 7 to 10 minutes.

* * * * * * * * *

# BEEF & LAMB

Combining beef with mac n' cheese is like cooking with a blank canvas since they are both so versatile and work so well together. Many of these recipes, like Meaty-Mac Loaf (page 119) or Mac Stuffed Peppers (page 124), use leftover beef. This way you can turn your remaining meat loaf, burgers, or whatever else into an entirely new dish.

# LONESTAR MAC

*Usually when I have barbecue, I accompany it with mac n' cheese—and the two often marry on my plate for one delicious bite. Why wait for that magic to happen on its own when I can create it whenever I want to by adding tender, juicy beef brisket to mac n' cheese?* **Serves 5**

1 box deluxe mac n' cheese

2 cups shredded cooked leftover beef brisket (or roast beef if you can't find brisket)

1 cup barbecue sauce

1 cup crispy onion straws

**1.** Cook the mac n' cheese as directed, and set it aside.

**2.** Heat the brisket in a medium pan over medium-low heat until heated through.

**3.** Mix together the beef brisket and barbecue sauce with the cooked mac n' cheese. Top with crispy onion straws.

• • • • • • • • •

# SWEDISH MEATBALLS N' MAC

*This recipe calls for smothering tiny, juicy meatballs in hot gravy and mac n' cheese, creating what I call cheesy, gravy goodness. The dish is inexpensive and easy to make.* **Serves 5**

1 box deluxe mac n' cheese

1 pound cooked miniature meatballs

1 cup jarred or leftover homemade beef gravy

**1.** Cook the mac n' cheese as directed, and set aside.

**2.** Cook the meatballs as directed. Mix the hot gravy and hot meatballs into the hot mac n' cheese, stirring until well combined.

• • • • • • • •

# REUBEN MAC

*I love taking an item that's usually a sandwich or an appetizer and turning it into a more filling meal. This recipe offers a perfect way to use leftover corned beef after St. Patrick's Day.* **Serves 4 or 5**

1 box deluxe mac n' cheese

1 pound chopped leftover cooked corned beef

1 cup Thousand Island or Russian dressing

2 cups shredded Swiss cheese (8 ounces), divided

1½ cups prepared sauerkraut

**1.** Preheat the oven to 425°F. Cook the mac n' cheese as directed.

**2.** Add the corned beef, dressing, and 1 cup Swiss cheese to the cooked mac n' cheese, stirring until well mixed.

**3.** Transfer to a 9 x 13-inch baking dish. Evenly distribute the remaining 1 cup Swiss cheese over top and bake uncovered until the cheese has started to brown. Remove from the oven and top with sauerkraut.

· · · · · · · · ·

# CHEERIO MAC

*This play on the classic English dish shepherd's pie features mac n' cheese instead of potatoes as a topping. Ground lamb is traditional, but I use ground beef because it's readily available at my grocery store.* **Serves 4 or 5**

1 box deluxe mac n' cheese

1 pound ground beef

1 medium onion, chopped

2 cloves garlic, finely chopped

½ cup frozen peas

½ cup frozen corn

1 teaspoon black pepper

1 teaspoon thyme

1 teaspoon garlic salt

1 cup shredded English cheddar cheese (4 ounces)

**1.** Preheat the oven to 400°F. Cook the mac n' cheese as directed, and set aside.

**2.** In a large deep nonstick skillet over medium-high heat, brown the ground beef, breaking it up with a wooden spoon. Cook until browned and cooked through, about 10 minutes. Drain off the fat.

**3.** Once the meat is cooked, turn the heat to low and stir in the onion and garlic. Continue to cook for an additional 10 minutes. Add the peas, corn, black pepper, thyme, and garlic salt, stirring well.

**4.** Transfer the ground beef and vegetable mixture to a deep casserole dish. Evenly distribute the cooked mac n' cheese over the top. Then top with the cheddar cheese. Bake uncovered until the cheese starts to brown, about 20 minutes.

• • • • • • • •

# PASTRAMI CASSEROLE

*There's nothing quite like visiting New York City after years of only seeing photos of it. And there's nothing quite like enjoying an authentic pastrami sandwich in the bustling city. That experience inspired this mac n' cheese dish.* **Serves 4 or 5**

1 box deluxe mac n' cheese

2 cups shredded Swiss cheese (8 ounces), divided

1½ pounds pastrami, chopped

drizzle of yellow mustard (optional)

**1.** Preheat the oven to 425°F. Cook the mac n' cheese as directed.

**2.** Add 1 cup Swiss cheese and the pastrami to the cooked mac n' cheese, stirring until well mixed. Transfer to a 9 x 13-inch baking dish. Sprinkle the remaining 1 cup Swiss cheese over the top and bake uncovered until the cheese melts. Remove from the oven and drizzle on mustard if desired.

• • • • • • • • •

# MEATY-MAC LOAF

*I got so tired of making meat loaf sandwiches to use up leftover meat loaf that I came up with this amazing recipe for combining it with mac n' cheese. The cheesy noodles work perfectly with meat loaf, and crispy onion straws make the dish special.* **Serves 5 or 6**

1 box mac n' cheese

2 cups crumbled leftover cooked meat loaf

½ cup bacon crumbles or bacon bits

1 cup ketchup

1 cup crispy onion straws

**1.** Cook the mac n' cheese as directed.

**2.** Add the meat loaf, bacon, and ketchup to the cooked mac n' cheese, stirring until well mixed. Top with crispy onion straws.

· · · · · · · · ·

# SALISBURY MAC

*The combination of cheese and gravy makes this dish a creamy comfort food. You can use a jarred product or homemade leftover beef gravy if you have it on hand.* **Serves 5 or 6**

1 box mac n' cheese

1½ cups jarred or leftover homemade beef gravy

2 cups chopped leftover cooked hamburger or meat loaf

½ cup chopped fresh chives

**1.** Cook the mac n' cheese as directed.

**2.** While the mac n' cheese is cooking, warm up the beef gravy in a small saucepan over low heat.

**3.** Add the hamburger or meat loaf and gravy to the hot, cooked mac n' cheese, stirring until well mixed. Sprinkle the chives over the top.

•  •  •  •  •  •  •  •  •

# FRENCH ONION MAC

*Anytime I have leftover beef stock from cooking a roast, I make French onion soup with it. For this French onion mac n' cheese, you can use store-bought beef broth.* **Serves 4 or 5**

1 box deluxe mac n' cheese

1 tablespoon olive oil

1 large sweet onion, thinly sliced

¼ cup red wine

½ cup beef broth

2 cups Swiss cheese or Gruyère cheese (8 ounces)

1 cup croutons of choice

**1.** Preheat the oven to 425°F. Cook the mac n' cheese as directed.

**2.** While the mac n' cheese is cooking, heat the olive oil in a large skillet over medium heat. Add the onion and cook, stirring occasionally, until translucent, about 10 minutes. Add the wine, increase the heat to high, and bring to a boil, then reduce the heat to low. Stir in the beef broth, cook over medium heat, and cook for another 10 minutes.

**3.** Add the wine and broth mixture to the hot mac n' cheese. Transfer to a 9 x 13-inch baking dish, and evenly distribute the Swiss cheese or Gruyère over the top. Cook uncovered until the cheese has melted, about 10 minutes. Remove from the oven and top with the croutons.

· · · · · · · · ·

# CHILI MAC

*I make chili in big portions in a crock pot. Adding leftover chili to mac n' cheese spices up the mac, making it more exciting. I've also made this recipe with chili cheese dip leftover after a party. Whether the chili is very spicy or not too piquant, with or without beans, or with meat or vegetarian, it works well in this dish.* **Serves 4 or 5**

1 box mac n' cheese

1½ cups leftover chili

1 cup shredded cheddar cheese (4 ounces)

1½ cups crumbled Fritos corn chips

**1.** Cook the mac n' cheese as directed.

**2.** While the mac n' cheese is cooking, heat up the leftover chili in a medium saucepan over medium-low heat.

**3.** Add the hot chili and cheddar cheese to the hot mac n' cheese. Stir until the ingredients are well mixed and the cheese has melted. For a crunch, top with Fritos.

•  •  •  •  •  •  •  •

# BEEF N' MAC STROGANOFF

*One of my favorite meals to make when it's cold outdoors, beef Stroganoff is hearty, thick, and rich. The creaminess of the cheese in the deluxe mac n' cheese adds a velvety texture.* **Serves 5 or 6**

2 tablespoons olive oil

1 medium onion, chopped

2 cups chopped mushrooms

1 cup jarred or leftover homemade beef gravy

2 cups shredded leftover cooked beef pot roast or other beef roast

⅛ teaspoon garlic salt

1 teaspoon black pepper

1 box deluxe mac n' cheese

½ cup sour cream

**1.** Heat the olive oil in a large deep skillet over medium-low heat. Add the onion and cook, stirring occasionally, for 5 minutes. Add the mushrooms and cook, stirring occasionally, until the mushrooms are tender and the onion translucent, about 10 minutes.

**2.** Add the gravy, beef, garlic salt, and black pepper to the vegetable mixture. Cook on low, until heated through, about 10 minutes.

**3.** While the meat mixture is cooking, prepare the mac n' cheese as directed. When both the mac n' cheese and the meat are properly cooked, mix them together, stirring well. Top each serving with a dollop of sour cream.

· · · · · · · · ·

# MAC STUFFED PEPPERS

*This recipe allows me to take any leftover meat loaf or hamburger and transform it into a new, fancier meal. I cook this dish in the oven so the peppers develop a slight sweetness that adds incredible flavor.*

**Serves 5 or 6**

1 box mac n' cheese

2 cups grated Asiago cheese (8 ounces), divided

2 cups chopped leftover cooked meat loaf or hamburger

½ medium onion, minced

3 cloves garlic, minced

3 (15-ounce) cans tomato sauce, divided

4 large green bell peppers

**1.** Preheat the oven to 400°F. Cook the mac n' cheese as directed.

**2.** In a large pot over medium heat, combine the cooked mac n' cheese, 1 cup Asiago cheese, leftover meat loaf or hamburger, onion, garlic, and 1 can tomato sauce. Cook for 10 minutes.

**3.** Hollow out the bell peppers by removing the stem and removing the membranes and seeds. Fill the peppers with the mac n' cheese mixture. Top the peppers with the remaining 1 cup Asiago cheese.

**4.** Transfer the peppers to a deep baking dish and cover with the remaining 2 cans of tomato sauce. Cover with aluminum foil and bake until the peppers reach the desired consistency, 35 to 45 minutes.

* * * * * * * * *

# ST. PADDY'S DAY TWIST

*Onions braised in Guinness beer are a perfect completion to this twist on a traditional Irish recipe. Whenever my family makes corned beef to celebrate St. Patrick's Day, there is always a good amount leftover. Using the leftovers in mac n' cheese opens the door to a whole new flavor and consistency.* **Serves 4 or 5**

1 tablespoon olive oil

2 medium onions, thinly sliced

1 box deluxe sharp cheddar mac n' cheese

1 cup Guinness beer

2 cups chopped leftover cooked corned beef

1 cup shredded Irish cheddar (4 ounces)

**1.** Heat the olive oil in a large skillet over medium heat. Add the onion and cook, stirring frequently, until translucent, 10 to 15 minutes.

**2.** While the onion is cooking, prepare the mac n' cheese as directed.

**3.** Add the beer to the cooked onion and bring to a boil. Reduce the heat to low and continue to cook for an additional 10 minutes.

**4.** Heat the corned beef in a medium saucepan just until heated through.

**5.** Mix together the hot corned beef, hot mac n' cheese, beer and onion mixture, and shredded cheddar cheese. Stir until well blended.

• • • • • • • • •

# SLOPPY JOE MAC

*If you want the taste of a sloppy joe without the mess or if you just want to revamp the dish, combine the sloppy joe fixings with mac n' cheese to create something different.* **Serves 4 or 5**

1 box mac n' cheese

1 pound ground beef

1 cup prepared barbecue sauce

1 (15-ounce) can sloppy joe sauce

2 cups potato chips (optional)

**1.** Cook the mac n' cheese as directed.

**2.** While the mac n' cheese is cooking, in a large nonstick skillet over medium high heat, brown the ground beef, breaking it up with a wooden spoon. Cook until browned and cooked through, about 10 minutes. Drain off the fat. Add the barbecue sauce and sloppy joe sauce, stirring until well mixed.

**3.** Stir the cooked mac n' cheese into the beef mixture until well combined. For a crunch, top each serving with potato chips.

· · · · · · · ·

# GRECIAN DELIGHT

*I crave gyro, but sometimes I just don't want it wrapped up in pita bread. Gyro meat is tender lamb roasted on a spit for hours and can be found in Greek restaurants as well as hot dog stands. Mac n' cheese is an unexpected alternative, and in this recipe it has all the traditional toppings.* **Serves 5**

1 box mac n' cheese

½ pound gyro meat, chopped

½ cup crumbled feta cheese (2 ounces)

½ tablespoon dried oregano

½ medium onion, chopped

½ cucumber, chopped

prepared tzatziki sauce (optional)

**1.** Cook the mac n' cheese as directed, and set aside.

**2.** To the pot of mac, add the chopped gyro meat, crumbled feta, oregano, onion, and cucumber. Stir until well blended. Top with tzatziki sauce, if using.

● ● ● ● ● ● ● ● ●

# APPENDIX

## Useful Conversions

| MEASURE | EQUIVALENT | METRIC |
|---|---|---|
| 1 teaspoon | -- | 5 milliliters |
| 1 tablespoon | 3 teaspoons | 14.8 milliliters |
| 1 cup | 16 tablespoons | 236.8 milliliters |
| 1 pint | 2 cups | 473.6 milliliters |
| 1 quart | 4 cups | 947.2 milliliters |
| 1 liter | 4 cups + 3½ tablespoons | 1000 milliliters |
| 1 ounce (dry) | 2 tablespoons | 28.35 grams |
| 1 pound | 16 ounces | 453.49 grams |
| 2.21 pounds | 35.3 ounces | 1 kilogram |
| 270°F / 350°F | -- | 132°C / 177°C |

# Volume Conversions

| U.S. | U.S. | METRIC |
| --- | --- | --- |
| (3 teaspoons) | 1 tablespoon, ½ fluid ounce | 15 ml |
| ¼ cup | 2 fluid ounces | 60 ml |
| ⅓ cup | 3 fluid ounces | 90 ml |
| ½ cup | 4 fluid ounces | 120 ml |
| ⅔ cup | 5 fluid ounces | 150 ml |
| ¾ cup | 6 fluid ounces | 180 ml |
| 1 cup | 8 fluid ounces | 240 ml |
| 2 cups | 16 fluid ounces | 480 ml |

# Weight Conversions

| U.S. | METRIC |
| --- | --- |
| ½ ounce | 15 grams |
| 1 ounce | 30 grams |
| 2 ounces | 60 grams |
| ¼ pound | 115 grams |
| ⅓ pound | 150 grams |
| ½ pound | 225 grams |
| ¾ pound | 350 grams |
| 1 pound | 450 grams |

# Temperature Conversions

| FAHRENHEIT (°F) | CELSIUS (°C) | GAS MARK |
| --- | --- | --- |
| 200°F | 95°C | 0 |
| 225°F | 110°C | ¼ |
| 250°F | 120°C | ½ |
| 275°F | 135°C | 1 |
| 300°F | 150°C | 2 |
| 325°F | 165°C | 3 |
| 350°F | 175°C | 4 |
| 375°F | 190°C | 5 |
| 400°F | 200°C | 6 |
| 425°F | 220°C | 7 |
| 450°F | 230°C | 8 |
| 475°F | 245°C | 9 |

# RECIPE INDEX